THE EVERYDAY HIGH PROTEIN HANDBOOK

First published in Great Britain in 2024 by Hodder Catalyst
An imprint of Hodder & Stoughton
An Hachette UK company

1

Copyright © Scott Baptie 2024
Photography © Georgie Glass 2024

A CIP catalogue record for this title is available from the British Library

Hardback ISBN 978 1 399 73228 4
eBook ISBN 978 1 399 73229 1

Publisher: Lauren Whelan
Senior Project Editor: Liv Nightingall
Copyeditor: Clare Sayer
Designer: Nathan Burton
Photography: Georgie Glass
Food Stylist: Angela Boggiano
Food Stylist Assistant: Daisy Hogg
Props Stylist: Morag Farquhar
Senior Production Controller: Susan Spratt

Colour origination by Alta Image London
Printed and bound in China by C&C Offset Printing Co., Ltd.

Hodder & Stoughton policy is to use papers that are natural, renewable and recyclable products and made from wood grown in sustainable forests. The logging and manufacturing processes are expected to conform to the environmental regulations of the country of origin.

Hodder Catalyst
Hodder & Stoughton Ltd
Carmelite House
50 Victoria Embankment
London
EC4Y 0DZ

www.hoddercatalyst.co.uk

The information and references contained herein are for informational purposes only. They are designed to support, not replace, any ongoing medical advice given by a healthcare professional and should not be construed as the giving of medical advice nor relied upon as a basis for any decision or action. Readers should consult their doctor before altering their diet, particularly if they are on a set diet prescribed by their doctor or dietitian. The calorie count for each recipe is an estimate only and may vary depending on the brand of ingredients used, and due to the natural biological variations in the composition of foods such as meat, fish, fruit and vegetables. It does not include the nutritional content of optional accompaniments recommended for taste/serving.

THE EVERYDAY HIGH PROTEIN HANDBOOK

80 delicious and easy
recipes for all the family

Scott Baptie

Photography by Georgie Glass

CONTENTS

3 FISH & VEG 130

4 SNACKS & DESSERTS 176

INTRODUCTION

Hello, or welcome back. If you've journeyed with me through the delicious pages of my first book, *The Ultimate High Protein Handbook*, if you've got my Food For Fitness app or if you already follow me on social media (@ScottBaptie), you know that I am all about bringing the benefits of high-protein eating to your dinner table with healthy, simple and scrumptious recipes.

If you've just picked this book up off the shelf and thought 'ooh, I like the look of that', firstly, thank you so much; secondly, the super-quick intro is that my name is Scott, I'm a sports nutritionist, former fitness cover model and high-protein recipe aficionado. Around 10 years ago, when I was stuck in a boring desk job, I set up a nutrition and fitness blog called Food For Fitness, posting workouts, meal plans and recipes. It evolved into a business and soon the high-protein recipes I was coming up with for my coaching clients became their favourite part about their meal plan. So much so that I knocked up my first High Protein Handbook as a digital PDF and that was really the first step that led us to where we are today.

In this book, my second culinary 'real book' adventure, *The Everyday High Protein Handbook*, I'm thrilled to bring you another collection of 80 recipes from around the globe that are not just mouth-watering but are also protein-packed powerhouses!

We've got 60 brand-new recipes that were created just for this book along with 20 of my most popular recipes that you might already be familiar with. On those 'follower favourite recipes' you'll find a handy QR code; if you scan it, you'll be taken to YouTube where you'll be able to see a full recipe video.

This book is for everyone – whether you're a fitness enthusiast looking to fuel your workouts, a busy parent seeking nutritious yet quick midweek meals, or simply someone aiming to boost their diet with more protein. My goal is to show you that eating healthier doesn't mean sacrificing flavour or spending hours in the kitchen. These recipes are designed to fit into your everyday life, offering a perfect blend of convenience and taste.

As with my first book, I've included all the macros and calorie counts for each recipe. And to make your health journey even smoother, you'll find a handy barcode with each recipe to scan directly into all the major food diary apps. It's all about making healthy eating as straightforward and enjoyable as possible.

For many of the recipes, I include some recommended sides and serving suggestions. To clarify, these side dishes have not been included as part of the nutritional information. The reason for this is that they are just suggestions, and how much or how little rice, for example, that you'd serve with a meal will depend on you. Including 50g of rice might be perfect for some people but for others trying to support recovery after exercise or build muscle, 50g wouldn't be sufficient. So, if I include something as 'To serve' and it's in the ingredients list, it will be included in the nutritional breakdown, but if something says '(optional)' or isn't in the ingredients list, then it won't. I do add some serving suggestions in the recipe methods, but it's up to you to decide if you want to follow them or not.

This book has been thoughtfully organised into sections based on different protein sources. Whether you're in the mood for chicken, beef or vegetarian options, you'll find a diverse range of recipes catering to your preferences. This layout makes it easy to navigate and choose meals that align with your dietary needs or cravings for the day.

So, let's turn the page and embark on this delicious high-protein journey together. Here's to good food, great health, and moments of joy around the dinner table.

Bon appétit!

Why high protein?

Superfoods aren't really a thing. But. . . if they were, protein would probably be right up there as the number 1 contender.

Protein and satiety

One of the main benefits of protein is that it can help keep hunger pangs at bay. When you eat it, certain hormones are released that send messages to your brain telling it that you're nice and full. In fact, protein is more satiating than carbohydrates or fats, meaning it can help you feel fuller for longer after eating. This can be a game-changer when it comes to sticking to a healthy eating routine and avoiding snacking between meals to stave off hunger.

Thermic effect of food (TEF)

Another reason why high-protein diets are the bee's knees is due to the thermic effect of food (TEF). TEF is essentially the amount of energy your body uses to digest, absorb and metabolise the nutrients in the food you eat. Protein has a higher thermic effect than carbohydrates or fats, meaning your body burns more calories when processing protein-rich foods. When you bump up your protein intake, you're essentially giving your metabolism a boost!

Muscle preservation

Another plus is that a higher protein intake can help you hold on to muscle. This is a good thing, even if you don't want to look like a bodybuilder! Muscle is more metabolically active than fat, meaning it burns more calories at rest. High-protein diets can help you preserve muscle mass during weight loss, ensuring that the weight you lose is primarily from fat stores. This isn't about losing fat to 'look' skinny; the end goal is to look and feel healthy, full of life and athletic, and holding on to muscle is the way to do this.

How much protein should I be eating?

How much protein you require depends on many factors, such as your goals, your body fat levels, your weight and so on. If you're simply trying to eat healthier, I wouldn't try and overanalyse this and fixate on a number (unless you're specifically tracking calories and/or macros). Just try and eat more protein any time you have a meal or snack. And hopefully by cooking the recipes in this book you'll be able to do just that.

Kitchen essentials

Just like in my last book, I am not going to tell you the obvious – that you should have a sieve, some pans, a chopping board, etc. I don't want 'filler' rubbish in this book, only stuff that will actually help you to eat better, so I want to get on to the recipes ASAP.

That being said, there are a few things that will make life easier for you.

Digital food scales
If you don't have these, get some. They're much more accurate than the old-school analogue ones with a moving needle.

Minced garlic and ginger
Because I can't be bothered faffing around peeling garlic and ginger, I use ready-made jars of garlic paste and ginger paste in all my recipes, as well as a combined garlic and ginger paste which contains about half and half minced garlic and ginger. This makes life super-speedy and you'll notice that when I'm using both garlic and ginger in a recipe the quantities are often the same, so you can just grab one jar. It's exactly what Indian restaurants use for speed and efficiency and you can usually find it in your local supermarket, or just jump online. If you are using whole garlic cloves, 1 medium-sized garlic clove will give you 5g of minced garlic.

One decent, sharp chef's knife
There are no recipes in this book that don't require some form of cutting, slicing or chopping beforehand. Therefore I would strongly recommend you invest in one good-quality chef's knife. Forget 20 different types of paring knife; just get one decent chef's knife that's around 18–20cm and you can pretty much use it for any chopping you require. If you look at my YouTube videos, you'll see I use one knife for everything. Look after it and sharpen it regularly and it'll be like a hot knife through butter.

That's it, three things. Easy, right?

Freezing food

Unlike many other cookbooks, I haven't included notes for each recipe on whether it can be frozen or not. This is generally because most of the things I cook are freezable, because I cook in bulk at home. There are four of us in the house, so I usually cook 6–8 portions of something and bung the rest in the freezer. Most of the recipes in this book will make about 4 portions but you can easily scale these up to fill the freezer for another day.

In general I wouldn't freeze recipes that have the rice or pasta included as part of the dish, so things like a pilaf, biryani or pasta mixed through meat and sauce would be a no-go. The reason is because I often find they don't reheat well and can go a bit stodgy. There are still quite a few myths around storing and reheating rice but the issue isn't the reheating, it's the storing. Specifically, you want to get rice into the fridge as soon as it's cooled down – don't leave it sitting around on a worktop for hours.

Some dairy-based sauces or coconut milk-based sauces can seem to disappear once they've been frozen; when you heat them up there is hardly any sauce, so I wouldn't freeze them. And finally, if you have a recipe that stirs through some form of low-fat dairy at the end then I wouldn't freeze that either. But like I said, most recipes CAN be frozen. Just make sure you reheat them so they're piping hot before you eat them again.

Now we've got all that out the way, let's get cooking!

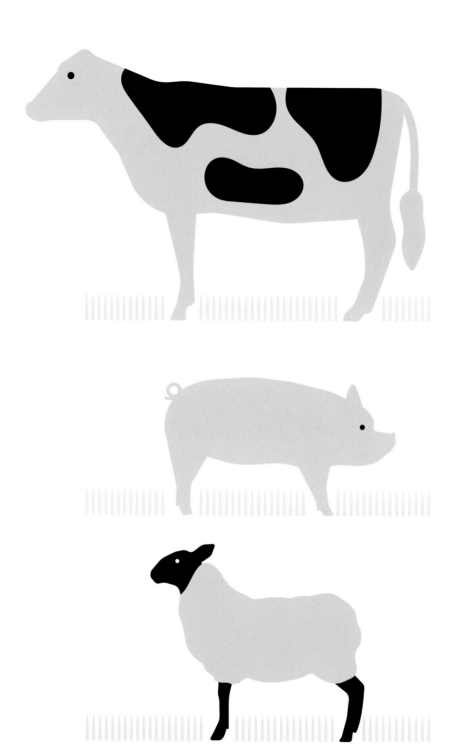

1

BEEF, PORK & LAMB

Sweet Potato Cottage Pie

PREP TIME: 20 MINS
COOK TIME: 2 HRS
SERVES: 8

For the mince
1 tbsp olive oil
2 onions, chopped
2 carrots, chopped
2 parsnips, chopped
15g minced garlic
1kg steak mince (5% fat)
2 tbsp flour
1 tbsp mixed herbs
1 tsp ground cinnamon
1 tbsp tomato purée
150ml red wine
500ml beef stock
2 tbsp balsamic vinegar

For the mash
1.5kg sweet potatoes, peeled and cut into large chunks
10g butter
1 tsp dried rosemary

We're reinventing a classic with this recipe. It's a comfort food twist you didn't even know you needed. This dish combines the savoury goodness of steak mince with the sweet touch of smooth, creamy sweet potatoes. When it comes out of the oven all bubbly and slightly crispy on top, you'll see (and smell) the magic I'm talking about!

Heat the olive oil in a large, non-stick pan over a medium heat, then throw in the onions, carrots, and parsnips and cook, stirring, for 10–15 minutes until the vegetables have softened. Add the garlic and fry for a further 30 seconds.

Add the mince and brown, breaking it up with a wooden spoon, then add the flour and stir through.

Add the mixed herbs, cinnamon, tomato purée, red wine, stock and balsamic vinegar and mix until everything is combined. Reduce the heat and simmer for 25–30 minutes until the sauce has thickened and you have a nice gravy that coats the mince and vegetables.

While the mince is simmering, bring a large pan of salted water to the boil and cook the sweet potatoes for about 20 minutes, or until soft. Drain, then return the sweet potatoes to the pan, add the butter and rosemary and mash until smooth.

Preheat the oven to 220ºC (200ºC fan)/425ºF/gas 7.

Once the meat is cooked, spoon it into a large ovenproof dish and cover it with the sweet potato mash. Bake in the hot oven for 30–40 minutes, or until it is bubbling and the sweet potato is starting to brown on top. Serve.

NUTRITIONAL INFO PER SERVING:
414 CALORIES
32g PROTEIN
45g CARBS
10g FAT

Food Diary Barcode:

Scan here for the recipe video

Korean Beef Bowls

PREP TIME: 15 MINS
COOK TIME: 15 MINS
SERVES: 4

1 tsp coconut oil
5g minced garlic
5g minced ginger
500g steak mince
30g honey
60ml soy sauce
10ml sesame oil
1 tsp chilli flakes
200ml water
1 tbsp cornflour
1 carrot, grated
3 spring onions, chopped

These are probably one of the easiest dishes you could make with a pack of mince. They're rich and tasty, and they take less than 15 minutes to cook, which makes them a favourite for a midweek meal. You've got protein-packed mince, zesty garlic, sweet honey, umami-rich soy sauce, fragrant sesame oil, spicy red pepper flakes and – to add a little crunch – some fresh spring onions and carrots.

Heat the coconut oil in a large pan over a medium heat, add the garlic and ginger and fry for about 1 minute until fragrant.

Add the mince to the pan and cooked until browned all over, breaking it up a bit with a wooden spoon.

Add the honey, soy sauce, sesame oil, chilli flakes, water and cornflour to a bowl and mix until fully combined. Pour this sauce over the mince, reduce the heat to low and simmer for 10 minutes.

Stir through the grated carrot and spring onions, then serve with rice, if liked.

NUTRITIONAL INFO PER SERVING:
273 CALORIES
30g PROTEIN
18g CARBS
9g FAT

Food Diary Barcode:

Scan here for the
recipe video

Bacheofe

PREP TIME: 20 MINS,
PLUS MARINATING
COOK TIME: 3 HRS
SERVES: 7

500g lean diced beef
500g lean diced pork
500g lean diced lamb
1 bottle of dry white wine
2 bouquets garnis
2 carrots, chopped
2 onions, chopped
2 leeks, chopped
20g minced garlic
800g potatoes, peeled and sliced
6 bacon medallions
Sea salt and black pepper
Flat-leaf parsley, to garnish

Embrace the hearty warmth of Alsatian cuisine with a traditional three-meat casserole that's the epitome of comfort food. This casserole would normally include a pig's trotter but I've skipped that for obvious reasons. We're still packing it with protein using beef, pork and lamb, it is a cinch to prepare and perfect for a lazy Sunday or a festive gathering. Serve with a handful of fresh parsley and some crusty bread. Cheers to simplicity and good taste!

Put the beef, pork and lamb into a large bowl along with the wine, bouquets garnis, carrots, onions, leeks and garlic. Cover and marinate in the fridge overnight for a minimum of 12 hours.

The next day, preheat the oven to 200°C (180°C fan)/400°F/gas 6.

Tip all of the ingredients that have been marinating, including the wine and bouquets garnis, into a large ovenproof casserole. Top with the potato slices (it doesn't matter if they overlap) and then lay the bacon on top of the potatoes. Put it into the oven and bake for 3 hours (there's no need to stir it during this time, as you want the potatoes to stay on top).

Serve garnished with some fresh parsley. As this is a complete meal (veg, meat and sauce), you don't need to add anything to it – maybe just some crusty bread to mop up the sauce.

NUTRITIONAL INFO PER SERVING:
494 CALORIES
68g PROTEIN
24g CARBS
14g FAT

Food Diary Barcode:

Argentinian Chimichurri Steak

PREP TIME: 20 MINS,
   PLUS MARINATING
COOK TIME: 10–15 MINS
SERVES: 4

For the chimichurri sauce
60ml extra virgin olive oil
15ml soy sauce
30ml red wine vinegar
15g minced garlic
1 small red chilli, deseeded and
   finely chopped (adjust to taste)
Large handful of coriander,
   finely chopped
Large handful of flat-leaf parsley,
   finely chopped
½ tsp dried oregano
¼ tsp smoked paprika
Sea salt and black pepper

For the steak
600g beef steaks (any cut)

Whisk yourself away to the bustling streets of Buenos Aires with this recipe. A delightful feast for the senses, it's a doddle to prepare and offers a dazzling blend of fresh herbs and bold spices. Whether you choose to marinate or not, each succulent slice promises a burst of flavour, guaranteed to liven up any gathering. Fire up your barbecue and ready your taste buds for a culinary adventure that's just a drizzle of chimichurri away!

In a bowl, combine all the ingredients for the chimichurri sauce. Mix well, then taste and adjust the seasoning if necessary. Set aside at room temperature to let the flavours mix. If making ahead, you can pop it in the fridge, but ensure it comes to room temperature before serving.

Take half of the chimichurri sauce and place it in a bowl or freezer bag. Add the steaks and turn in the marinade to make sure they're well-coated, then transfer to the fridge to marinate for 1–3 hours. This step infuses more flavour into the steaks, but if you are short on time, you can skip this step and just season the steaks before cooking.

If you are using a barbecue, preheat it to a high heat; if using a pan, place it over high heat and fry the steaks to your desired level of doneness.

Once done, remove the steaks from the heat and let them rest for about 5 minutes. This helps the juices redistribute, ensuring a juicy steak. Serve the steaks with the reserved chimichurri sauce drizzled on top or on the side.

NUTRITIONAL INFO PER SERVING:
325 CALORIES
32g PROTEIN
2g CARBS
21g FAT

Food Diary Barcode:

Cuban Ropa Vieja

PREP TIME: 15 MINS
COOK TIME: 4–5 HRS
SERVES: 6

1 tbsp oil
2 onions, thinly sliced
1 red pepper, thinly sliced
1 yellow pepper, thinly sliced
20g minced garlic
2 tsp ground cumin
1 tsp ground paprika
½ tsp ground turmeric
1 x 400g tin of chopped tomatoes
250ml beef stock
2 tbsp tomato purée
2 bay leaves
1 tbsp white wine vinegar
1kg beef brisket, cut into quarters
100g green olives, pitted
 and sliced
Sea salt and black pepper

This recipe is one of my favourites in this book – so you better like it! It transforms the humble beef brisket into a tender, shredded masterpiece, simmered gently with peppers, onions and a medley of spices that will make you think you're wandering down the streets of Havana.

Preheat the oven to 180ºC (160ºC fan)/320ºF/gas 3.

Heat the oil in a large casserole over a medium-high heat and sauté the onions and peppers until soft and translucent, about 5 minutes. Add the garlic, ground cumin, paprika and turmeric and cook for another minute.

Add the chopped tomatoes, beef stock, tomato purée, bay leaves, ½ teaspoon of salt and the white wine vinegar. Stir well.

Add the beef to the mixture and spoon some sauce over it. Cover the casserole and place it in the oven for about 4 hours.

After 4 hours, once the beef is tender, remove it from the dish and place it on a chopping board. Use two forks to shred the meat, then return the shredded meat to the pot with the olives. Stir everything well and let it cook for another 20 minutes. Check the seasoning and adjust with salt and pepper as needed.

Serve over rice, garnished with chopped coriander.

NUTRITIONAL INFO PER SERVING:
362 CALORIES
39g PROTEIN
11g CARBS
18g FAT

Food Diary Barcode:

Haggis Burger

PREP TIME: 5 MINS
COOK TIME: 10 MINS
MAKES: 6 BURGERS

250g haggis or black pudding
500g beef mince (5% fat)

This is the shortest recipe I've ever written and likely ever will, unless butter on toast is to feature in a future book! Seriously though, it needs nothing else added. The fat and spices from the haggis combined with the beef mince is all you need. Ridiculously simple.

Remove the haggis or black pudding from its casing and mix with the beef mince until fully combined. Shape into 6 burgers, then fry, grill or barbecue. You could have these on their own with veg or make up some traditional burgers.

NUTRITIONAL INFO PER SERVING:
211 CALORIES
22g PROTEIN
6g CARBS
11g FAT

Food Diary Barcode:

Lomo Saltado

PREP TIME: 15 MINS,
PLUS MARINATING
COOK TIME: 10 MINS
SERVES: 4

600g thin beef steak, sliced
3 tbsp dark soy sauce
2 tbsp white or red wine vinegar
20g minced garlic
1 tsp ground cumin
2 tsp oil
2 onions, cut into wedges
2 peppers (preferably red
 and yellow), sliced
3 tomatoes, cut into wedges
2 chillies (adjust to your heat
 preference), sliced
Sea salt and black pepper
400g chips, cooked to your liking
Chopped coriander, to garnish

This Peruvian staple brings together tender beef and crisp vegetables in a quick stir-fry. Seasoned with tasty spices and a hint of soy sauce, it's a straightforward weeknight meal that packs a flavour punch. Served with a side of chips (winner) and rice, it's a balanced plate that offers a taste of Peru's culinary diversity. Remember to cook it fast and hot to keep the ingredients at their best, and finish with a sprinkle of coriander for a fresh contrast.

In a bowl, combine the sliced beef with 2 tablespoons of the soy sauce, the vinegar, garlic and cumin and season with salt and pepper. Mix well and set aside for about 15–20 minutes.

Heat 1 teaspoon of the oil in a large pan or wok over a high heat. Add the marinated beef slices, making sure you don't overcrowd the pan. Fry until the beef is browned but still slightly pink in the middle. Remove from the pan and set aside.

Add the remaining teaspoon of oil to the same pan, then add the onions and peppers. Stir-fry for 2–3 minutes until they begin to soften but retain a bit of crunch. Add the tomatoes, chillies and the remaining tablespoon of soy sauce. Stir-fry for another 2 minutes, then return the cooked beef to the pan. Toss everything together to combine.

Serve the lomo saltado over the cooked chips on a plate and garnish with chopped coriander. Typically, this dish is also accompanied by cooked rice on the side, allowing you to enjoy the juices from the stir-fry.

TIPS

This dish is meant to be cooked quickly over a high heat, retaining the freshness of the ingredients while achieving a good char.

For a more authentic flavour, if available, use Peruvian yellow chilli paste (aji amarillo) in place of the sliced chillies.

NUTRITIONAL INFO PER SERVING:
577 CALORIES
35g PROTEIN
44g CARBS
29g FAT

Food Diary Barcode:

632 CALORIES per serving

Venison Steaks with Celeriac Mash & Blackberry Gravy

PREP TIME: 20 MINS
COOK TIME: 35 MINS
SERVES: 2

150g blackberries
250ml beef stock
1 tbsp redcurrant jelly
35g butter
250g celeriac, peeled and chopped
400g potatoes, peeled and chopped
60ml milk
Bunch of chives, finely chopped
2 venison steaks
1 tbsp olive oil
Sea salt and black pepper

Tuck into a dish that artfully combines rustic charm with gourmet flair. This meal is a celebration of robust flavours, featuring tender venison steaks that are perfectly complemented by the earthy tones of celeriac mash and the sweet tartness of blackberry gravy.

Put the blackberries into a small saucepan (reserving a few to garnish) with the stock, redcurrant jelly and 10g of the butter. Place over a medium heat and simmer until reduced by half – this will take about 15 minutes.

Add the celeriac to another saucepan, cover with cold water and bring to the boil. Simmer for about 5 minutes, then add the potatoes and cook for a further 20 minutes until very soft and cooked through. Drain well, then return to the saucepan with the remaining butter and the milk and mash until smooth and creamy. Season with salt and pepper to taste, then stir through the chives. Keep warm while you cook the venison.

Season the steaks well with salt and pepper. Heat the oil in a heavy-based frying pan until hot and fry the venison steaks for about 2 minutes each side for rare, 3 minutes each side for medium, or 4 minutes each side for well done. Set aside and cover with foil to keep warm.

Slice the venison into thick slices and serve with the mash, gravy and reserved blackberries, plus green beans or tenderstem broccoli, if you like.

NUTRITIONAL INFO PER SERVING:
632 CALORIES
35g PROTEIN
51g CARBS
32g FAT

Food Diary Barcode:

Pakistani Nihari

PREP TIME: 30 MINS
COOK TIME: 3½ HRS
SERVES: 5

1 tbsp coconut oil
1 tsp fennel seeds
2 star anise
2 cardamom pods, split open
2 large onions, thinly sliced
1kg lean diced beef
30g minced garlic
30g minced ginger
3–4 green chillies, slit
2 tsp chilli powder
1 tsp ground turmeric
1 tsp ground cumin
2 bay leaves
30g cornflour
750ml beef stock
1 tsp garam masala
Chopped coriander leaves,
    to garnish
Sliced ginger slices, to garnish
Lemon wedges, to serve

Nihari is a deeply flavourful beef stew. The dish starts with a base of fragrant spices like fennel, star anise and cardamom, all sizzling in coconut oil. Garlic, ginger and a load of amazing spices then envelop the meat, which is then slow-cooked to tender perfection. Served alongside naan or rice with a squeeze of lemon, it's a meal that's as nourishing as it is satisfying.

Preheat the oven to 180ºC (160ºC fan)/350ºF/gas 4.

Heat the oil in a large casserole over a medium heat. Add the fennel seeds, star anise and cardamom pods and fry for 15–30 seconds, just long enough to allow the flavours to infuse into the oil. Add the sliced onions and fry until softened.

Add the meat and brown all over (you may need to do this in batches), then add the garlic, ginger, green chillies, ground spices and bay leaves. Stir well to coat the meat in the spices and fry for a further minute.

Add the cornflour and stir through, then add the beef stock. Cover with a lid, then place into the oven for about 3 hours; check it occasionally and top up with more water if it looks a little dry.

Just before serving, sprinkle over the garam masala and stir gently. Serve in deep bowls, garnished with chopped coriander and ginger slices. Serve with naan or steamed rice, accompanied by lemon wedges for squeezing over.

NUTRITIONAL INFO PER SERVING:
362 CALORIES
46g PROTEIN
13g CARBS
14g FAT

Food Diary Barcode:

Vietnamese Shaking Beef

**PREP TIME: 15 MINS,
    PLUS MARINATING**
COOK TIME: 5 MINS
SERVINGS: 3

For the beef marinade
500g frying steak, sliced
5g minced garlic
5g minced ginger
1 tbsp dark soy sauce
1 tbsp fish sauce
1 tbsp oyster or hoisin sauce
1 tsp brown sugar
Good grinding of black pepper

For the vinaigrette
40ml rice vinegar
10g brown sugar
15ml neutral oil
10g minced garlic
1 red chilli, deseeded
    and finely chopped
1 tbsp fish sauce
10ml dark soy sauce

Venture into the bustling streets of Hanoi with this recipe, where beef is marinated in a tantalising mix of soy, fish and oyster sauces, with hints of garlic and ginger, then quickly seared to perfection. It's then drizzled with a homemade vinaigrette that balances tangy rice vinegar with the sweetness of sugar and the heat of chilli. Serve over a crisp salad for a refreshing, light meal that's packed with bold Vietnamese character.

Mix all the marinade ingredients together in a large bowl, then cover and pop it into the fridge for at least 30 minutes, but overnight is better.

Whisk together all the vinaigrette ingredients in a bowl.

When you are ready to cook, place a wok over a high heat and add the beef (you won't need any oil if your wok is non-stick). Fry the beef for a few minutes until it starts to crisp up.

Serve the beef on top of a salad of your choice and drizzle the vinaigrette over it.

NUTRITIONAL INFO PER SERVING:
260 CALORIES
38g PROTEIN
9g CARBS
8g FAT

Food Diary Barcode:

Beef Stifado

PREP TIME: 2 MINS
COOK TIME: 3 HRS
SERVES: 6

20 shallots, peeled but left whole
4 garlic cloves, peeled
   but left whole
400g passata
1 large glass of red wine
½ tsp ground cinnamon
½ tsp ground nutmeg
1 tsp dried oregano
2 tbsp red wine vinegar
1 tsp salt
1 tsp black pepper
4 whole cloves
2 bay leaves
3 small sprigs of rosemary
1kg lean diced beef

This hearty, traditional Greek stifado is made with tender beef, shallots and a flavourful tomato and red wine sauce, spiced with cinnamon and cloves. Perfect for cold winter nights, this dish is sure to warm you up and satisfy your taste buds.

Preheat the oven to 180°C (160°C fan)/350°F/gas 4.

Put all the ingredients into a casserole dish and mix through.

Cover the dish and place it in the oven for about 3 hours (give it a mix halfway through cooking). Serve with rice, orzo or potatoes.

NUTRITIONAL INFO PER SERVING:
271 CALORIES
40g PROTEIN
12g CARBS
7g FAT

Food Diary Barcode:

Scan here for the
recipe video

Braised Chinese Beef Casserole with Fennel & Lime Slaw

PREP TIME: 25 MINS
COOK TIME: 2½ HRS
SERVES: 6

2 tbsp coconut oil

1kg good-quality stewing beef,
  such as shin

1 large onion, chopped

15g minced garlic

15g minced ginger

1½ tbsp Szechuan peppercorns

25g plain flour, plus extra for dusting

2 tbsp tomato purée

4 medium potatoes,
  cut into large cubes

3 carrots, cut into large pieces

4 star anise

1 cinnamon stick

100ml light soy sauce

3 whole dried red chillies

2 tbsp dark muscovado sugar

For the fennel and lime coleslaw

1 large carrot, finely shredded
  or roughly grated

4 spring onions, halved
  and shredded

100g mangetout, thinly sliced

1 fennel bulb, trimmed and
  very thinly sliced

28g pack of fresh coriander,
  roughly chopped

Small bunch of fresh mint,
  roughly, chopped

Juice of 1 large lime

2 tbsp olive oil

Pinch of salt

Here beef – slow-cooked until tender – bathes in a sauce fragrant with Szechuan peppercorns, star anise and cinnamon, creating a symphony of warm spices. Paired with a crisp fennel and lime slaw that offers a refreshing contrast, the dish balances the hearty with the light. Served with coconut rice, it's a meal that's perfect for a family dinner or to impress at a social gathering.

Heat 1 tablespoon of the oil in a large flameproof casserole over a high heat. Working in batches, brown the meat all over for a few minutes, then remove from the pan and set aside.

Add the onion, garlic and ginger to the pan and cook over a medium heat for a few minutes until starting to soften.

Finely crush the Szechuan peppercorns in a pestle and mortar, then stir in the flour. Add the spiced flour to the casserole and cook for a few seconds, then return the meat and toss everything together.

Add the remaining ingredients to the casserole, then cover with 600ml water. Bring to a simmer, then cook, covered, over a very low heat for 2–2½ hours until the meat is very tender and the sauce is thickened and glossy.

Meanwhile, make the coleslaw. Put the carrot, spring onions, mangetout, fennel, coriander and mint in a large bowl and mix together well. In a small bowl mix together the lime juice, olive oil and salt, then pour over the vegetables and toss together well. Leave to sit for a few minutes before serving.

Serve the casserole with the coleslaw and some coconut rice, if liked.

NUTRITIONAL INFO PER SERVING:
475 CALORIES
40g PROTEIN
36g CARBS
19g FAT

Food Diary Barcode:

Cheesy One-Pan Mexican Beef

PREP TIME: 10 MINS
COOK TIME: 30 MINS
SERVES: 4

1 tbsp oil
1 red pepper, chopped
1 red onion, sliced
10g minced garlic
2 tbsp fajita seasoning
500g lean steak mince
300g rice (dried weight)
1 x 400g tin of chopped tomatoes
700ml beef stock (made with
    1 stock cube)
60g low-fat Cheddar, grated
Handful of fresh coriander

This is a treat that is guaranteed to level up your dinner plans: it's a flavour-packed, one-pan meal that is perfect for those busy weeknights when you want something that everyone will love but that is super quick to make and easy to clean up!

Heat the oil in a large pan over a medium heat, add the red pepper and onion and fry for a few minutes until softened.

Add the garlic and fajita seasoning and fry for 30 seconds, stirring, then add the mince and brown for a few more minutes, breaking up the mince with a wooden spoon.

Add the rice and stir to get it all coated in the mince mixture, then add the chopped tomatoes and stock. Reduce the heat to medium-low, cover with a lid and simmer for about 20 minutes, stirring once or twice. (The rice doesn't need to be fully cooked at this point; it should still be firm-ish.)

Sprinkle the cheese on top and turn off the heat but keep the pan on the hob, cover and allow the steam to continue to cook the rice for a further 3–5 minutes.

Scatter over the coriander, serve and enjoy!

NUTRITIONAL INFO PER SERVING:
447 CALORIES
31g PROTEIN
56g CARBS
11g FAT

Food Diary Barcode:

Scan here for the
recipe video

Chipotle Steak Bowl

PREP TIME: 15 MINS,
PLUS MARINATING
COOK TIME: 15 MINS
SERVINGS: 4

10g minced garlic
1 tsp smoked paprika
1 tsp ground cumin
1 tsp dried oregano
2 tsp chipotle paste
Juice of 1 lime
2 tbsp olive oil
600g frying steak, sliced
Sea salt and black pepper

For the green avocado
yoghurt sauce
1 ripe avocado
150g Greek yoghurt
Handful of coriander
Juice of 1 lime
1 small garlic clove
2 tbsp olive oil
1–2 tbsp water (if needed,
    to thin the sauce)

The punchy chipotle and bright zing of lime create a marinade that's a total doozie and all kinds of delicious. Paired with the creamy, dreamy green avocado yoghurt sauce, it's a match made in culinary heaven. Whether you're after a quick dinner fix or prepping for a lively gathering, this dish is a sure-fire way to spice things up. So plate up, drizzle generously, and let the good times roll!

In a bowl, combine the minced garlic, smoked paprika, ground cumin, oregano, chipotle paste, lime juice and olive oil. Season with salt and pepper and stir until well mixed. Add the steak to the marinade, turning to ensure it's fully coated. Let it marinate for at least 30 minutes, or up to 24 hours for deeper flavour.

When you're ready to cook, place a frying pan over a high heat. Remove the steak from the marinade, letting excess marinade drip off. Add the steak to the hot pan and cook for a couple of a minutes. Let it rest for a few minutes while you make the sauce.

Scoop out the flesh of the avocado and put it in a blender or food processor. Add the Greek yoghurt, coriander, lime juice, garlic and olive oil and season with salt and pepper. Blend until smooth, adding a little water if needed to get the sauce to a drizzling consistency.

Serve the steak with rice and top with the green sauce. This would also go well with some tortilla chips and salsa.

NUTRITIONAL INFO PER SERVING:
373 CALORIES
39g PROTEIN
7g CARBS
21g FAT

Food Diary Barcode:

Slow Cooker Beef Rendang

PREP TIME: 15 MINS
COOK TIME: 8 HRS
SERVES: 5

1kg lean beef, cut into chunks
1 x 400ml tin of coconut milk
1 star anise
1 cinnamon stick
2 tsp tamarind paste
1 tbsp brown sugar
1 tsp salt
30g cornflour
Coriander leaves, to garnish

For the spice paste
2 red chillies
½ red onion
20g minced ginger
20g minced garlic
20g minced lemongrass
1 tsp ground turmeric
1 tsp ground coriander
1 tsp ground cumin
1 tbsp lime juice
1 tbsp oil

Beef rendang is a sumptuous Indonesian curry that's slow-cooked to perfection. Its depth of flavour comes from a homemade paste, blending aromatic flavours like lemongrass, ginger and chillies with earthy spices such as turmeric and cumin. The beef, cooked in this paste and simmered in coconut milk, becomes meltingly tender. Serve over jasmine rice, with a side of pickled vegetables or a simple cucumber salad to cut through the richness.

Start by preparing the spice paste. Add all the ingredients to a blender and blitz until smooth.

Place a pan over a medium heat, add the spice paste and cook for 2–3 minutes before tipping it into the slow cooker.

Add all the remaining ingredients, except the coriander leaves, to the slow cooker, cover and cook on low for 8 hours.

Scatter over the coriander leaves and serve with rice.

NUTRITIONAL INFO PER SERVING:
465 CALORIES
44g PROTEIN
16g CARBS
25g FAT

Food Diary Barcode:

South African Bobotie

PREP TIME: 10 MINS
COOK TIME: 50 MINS
SERVES: 4

2 slices of white bread
400ml semi-skimmed milk
1 tbsp coconut oil
2 onions, finely chopped
15g minced garlic
2 tbsp curry powder
1 tsp ground turmeric
750g beef mince (5% fat)
60g sultanas or raisins
30g mango chutney
1 tbsp Worcestershire sauce
30g toasted flaked almonds
2 large eggs
Pinch of ground turmeric
    or saffron, for colour
Sea salt and black pepper
Bay leaves or lemon leaves,
    to garnish

This may be one of my favourite recipes in the book. Bobotie is like a meatloaf that blends sweet and savoury, with a richly spiced minced meat base and a golden topping, sort of like a moussaka. The addition of sultanas gives a subtle sweetness that contrasts with the deep, savoury flavours of the curry powder and turmeric. This would normally be served with yellow rice and perhaps a side of tangy chutney.

Preheat the oven to 180°C (160°C fan)/350°F/gas 4.

Start by soaking the bread slices in the milk in a bowl until they go mushy (yes, this sounds weird, but trust me). Set aside.

Heat the coconut oil in a large frying pan over a medium-high heat. Add the onions and cook until soft and translucent, then add the garlic, curry powder and turmeric and fry for a further minute. Add the mince and cook until browned, breaking it up with a wooden spoon.

Squeeze the milk from the bread, reserving the milk for later. Crumble the soaked bread into the meat mixture and stir in the sultanas or raisins, mango chutney, Worcestershire sauce and almonds. Season with salt and plenty of pepper.

Reduce the heat to medium-low, cover and cook the mixture for about 10 minutes, then remove from heat and transfer to a greased, ovenproof dish, pressing it down with the back of a spoon.

In a bowl, whisk together the eggs, reserved milk and a pinch of turmeric or saffron. Pour this mixture over the meat in the dish, then top with a few bay leaves or lemon leaves.

Bake in the oven for 30–35 minutes, or until the topping is set and golden. Let the bobotie rest for a few minutes before serving.

NUTRITIONAL INFO PER SERVING:
592 CALORIES
53g PROTEIN
41g CARBS
24g FAT

Food Diary Barcode:

326
CALORIES
per serving

Slow Cooker Bolognese

PREP TIME: 15 MINS
COOK TIME: 6 HRS 10 MINS
SERVES: 7

1 tsp olive oil
6 bacon medallions, chopped
2 onions, chopped
10g minced garlic
500g beef mince (5% fat)
500g pork mince (5% fat)
500g passata
2 carrots, chopped
1 tbsp cornflour
175ml wine (any colour)
1 tbsp mixed herbs
½ tsp black pepper

This slow cooker bolognese is hearty and comforting – the perfect dish for a cosy weeknight dinner. I love using the slow cooker for mince dishes. Have you noticed how when you cook a recipe with mince, it always tastes better the next day once the mince has had a chance to absorb the flavours from the sauce? Cooking mince in a slow cooker gives you that delicious rich taste on day one, straight out of the pot.

Heat the olive oil in a frying pan over a medium heat and cook the bacon, onions and garlic for about 5 minutes until the bacon is crisp and the onion is golden brown.

Increase the heat slightly and, working in batches, add the mince to the frying pan and cook until browned. Transfer the browned mince to the slow cooker, draining any excess fat.

Tip all the remaining ingredients into the slow cooker, mix through, cover with the lid and cook on low for 6 hours or medium for 4 hours. Serve with spaghetti, if liked.

NUTRITIONAL INFO PER SERVING:
326 CALORIES
47g PROTEIN
12g CARBS
10g FAT

Food Diary Barcode:

Scan here for the
recipe video

Irish Stew

PREP TIME: 15 MINS
COOK TIME: 2½ HRS
SERVES: 5

2 tbsp oil
1kg diced lamb or beef
2 large onions, chopped
    into chunks
3 carrots, peeled and sliced
    into rounds
1 leek, sliced
1 litre lamb or beef stock
2 bay leaves
Few sprigs of fresh thyme
    (or 1 tsp dried thyme)
800g potatoes, peeled and
    sliced into 1cm disks
1 tbsp butter
Sea salt and black pepper
Chopped parsley, to garnish

Irish stew is a dish that embodies the essence of hearty home cooking – flavoursome pieces of lamb are simmered with robust root vegetables in a rich, savoury stock. Topped with golden potatoes that have soaked up all the flavours of the stew beneath them, each spoonful is a tribute to the unpretentious goodness of Irish cuisine. Best enjoyed with a slice of crusty bread.

Preheat the oven to 180°C (160°C fan)/350°F/gas 4.

Heat 1 tablespoon of the oil in a large casserole over a medium heat. Add the lamb pieces and brown them on all sides, then remove from the pan and set aside.

Add the remaining oil to the pan, then add the onions, carrots and leek, sautéing them until translucent. Return the lamb to the pan, then add the stock, bay leaves and thyme and season to taste with salt and pepper.

Arrange the sliced potatoes on top, dab them with the butter and season again with salt and pepper. Cover with a lid and place in the oven for 1½–2 hours. Remove the lid and return to the oven for a further 10–15 minutes to allow the potatoes to get a bit more colour – alternatively you can pop it, uncovered, under a hot grill.

Check the seasoning and adjust with more salt and pepper if needed. Ladle the stew into bowls (remove the bay leaves and thyme sprigs if you used fresh thyme as you serve) and garnish with chopped parsley. Serve with crusty bread on the side.

NOTES

The beauty of Irish stew is in its simplicity.
However, you can make variations if you like:

• Add other root vegetables, such as parsnip,
  sweet potato, celeriac.

• Some people also like to add a splash of stout
  (like Guinness) for a richer depth of flavour.

• While lamb is traditional, beef can
  be used instead.

NUTRITIONAL INFO PER SERVING:
507 CALORIES
50g PROTEIN
34g CARBS
19g FAT

Food Diary Barcode:

Guyanese Pepperpot

PREP TIME: 10 MINS
COOK TIME: 3 HRS
SERVES: 4

2 tbsp coconut oil
1kg lean diced beef
2 large onions, finely chopped
30g minced garlic
2 Scotch bonnet peppers
    or 1 red chilli, deseeded and
    finely chopped (adjust to
    your heat preference)
2 tbsp cornflour
100ml dark treacle
2 tbsp soy sauce
1 tbsp Worcestershire sauce
2 cinnamon sticks
2 sprigs of fresh thyme
    (or 1 tsp dried thyme)
½ tsp freshly ground black pepper
2 bay leaves
800ml beef stock
Chopped spring onions and
    coriander, to garnish

The combination of succulent beef, infused with the sweet and spicy notes of treacle and Scotch bonnet peppers, simmers slowly to create a rich and delicious stew. Pepperpot is traditionally made around Christmas time in Guyana and gets better in flavour when left to sit for a day or two, so if you have the time, make it a day in advance. This would traditionally be made with cassareep, a thick, black liquid made from cassava root, but as you're unlikely to find it in your local supermarket, I've made a few tweaks to try and replicate the flavour.

Preheat the oven to 180°C (160°C fan)/350°F/gas 4.

Heat the oil in a large casserole over a high heat. Working in batches, add the beef pieces and brown them on all sides. Remove from the casserole and set aside.

In the same pan, reduce the heat to medium-high, add the chopped onions and sauté until translucent. Add the garlic and chillies, cooking for another minute until fragrant. Stir in the cornflour, ensuring the onions get a good coating.

Add the treacle, soy sauce, Worcestershire sauce, cinnamon sticks, thyme, black pepper, bay leaves and stock, stirring to combine.

Return the browned meat to the pan and bring the mixture to a gentle boil, then cover and place in the oven for 2½–3 hours, by which time the meat should become incredibly tender and the sauce should thicken slightly.

Once ready, ladle the pepperpot into bowls and garnish with chopped spring onions and coriander, if desired. Pepperpot is traditionally served with bread (like homemade plait bread) or rice, which is perfect for soaking up the rich sauce.

NUTRITIONAL INFO PER SERVING:
540 CALORIES
58g PROTEIN
32g CARBS
20g FAT

Food Diary Barcode:

Harissa Meatballs

PREP TIME: 20 MINS
COOK TIME: 20 MINS
SERVES: 4

1 tsp olive oil, plus extra for
    frying the meatballs
1 onion, finely chopped
10g minced garlic
1 tsp ground cumin
1 tsp ground coriander
½ tsp ground cinnamon
2 tsp harissa paste (or to taste)
1 egg
½ tsp salt
500g lean lamb mince
80g breadcrumbs
Handful of parsley, finely
    chopped, plus a few
    leaves to garnish
Handful of mint, finely chopped,
    plus a few leaves to garnish

For the yoghurt sauce
200g Greek yoghurt
1 tsp harissa paste
5g minced garlic
1 tbsp lemon juice
Sea salt

Ignite your palate with these beauties, where North African spices meet the timeless comfort of the classic meatball. Infused with the vibrancy of harissa, a whisper of cinnamon and the warmth of cumin and coriander, each bite is packed with flavour. Fresh herbs like parsley and mint add a burst of freshness to the already winning combination of spice and succulence. Paired with a tangy, harissa-spiked yoghurt sauce, this dish is perfect for a midweek dinner.

Heat the olive oil in a frying pan over a medium heat and fry the onion until it starts to turn golden brown. Add the garlic, cumin, coriander, cinnamon and harissa paste and fry for a further 30 seconds to 1 minute.

Tip the mixture from the frying pan into a large mixing bowl. Add the egg, salt, lamb mince, breadcrumbs, parsley and mint. Mix everything through, then shape into about 16 meatballs.

Heat a drizzle of oil in a large frying pan and pan-fry the meatballs over a medium heat until cooked fully. (Alternatively, cook them in an air fryer at 190°C for 12–14 minutes.)

While the meatballs are cooking, in a small bowl mix together the Greek yoghurt, harissa, garlic, lemon juice and a pinch of salt.

Place the meatballs on a serving dish and serve hot with the yoghurt sauce on the side. Garnish with a few fresh herbs if desired.

NUTRITIONAL INFO PER SERVING:
331 CALORIES
34g PROTEIN
15g CARBS
15g FAT

Food Diary Barcode:

North African-Inspired Lamb & Vegetable Stew

PREP TIME: 20 MINS
COOK TIME: 2 HRS
SERVES: 6

1 tbsp oil
800g lean lamb or beef,
    cut into chunks
2 large onions, finely chopped
15g minced garlic
15g minced ginger
2 tsp harissa paste
2 tsp ground cumin
1 tsp ground coriander
½ tsp ground cinnamon
¼ tsp ground turmeric
1.5 litres lamb or chicken stock
2 carrots, sliced into rounds
2 courgettes, sliced
    into half-moons
1 turnip, peeled and diced
200g butternut squash or
    pumpkin, peeled and diced
100g chickpeas (drained weight)
70g raisins or sultanas
Sea salt and black pepper
Chopped coriander and
    parsley, to garnish

This is a heart-warming pot loaded with the earthy goodness of root vegetables and the succulent richness of lamb, simmered gently in a sauce fragrant with spices. Each spoonful is infused with the vibrant kick of harissa, the warm depths of cumin and coriander, and a hint of sweetness from raisins, creating layers of complex flavours that are the hallmark of North African cuisine.

Heat the oil in a large saucepan over a medium heat. Working in batches, add the chunks of meat and brown them on all sides. Remove and set aside.

Add the onions to the same pan and fry them until softened, then add the garlic, ginger, harissa and ground spices and cook for another 2 minutes.

Return the browned meat to the pot, pour in the stock and season with salt and pepper. Bring to the boil, then reduce to a simmer, cover and cook for 45 minutes.

After 45 minutes, add the carrots, courgettes, turnip, butternut squash and chickpeas. Continue to simmer for another 45–60 minutes, or until the vegetables and meat are tender, adding the raisins or sultanas for the last 10 minutes of cooking. Serve garnished with chopped coriander and parsley, as well as rice or couscous, if liked.

NUTRITIONAL INFO PER SERVING:
331 CALORIES
33g PROTEIN
25g CARBS
11g FAT

Food Diary Barcode:

Pork Larb with Aubergine

PREP TIME: 10 MINS
COOK TIME: 15 MINS
SERVES: 4

2 tbsp olive oil
1 medium aubergine, cubed
1 bunch of spring onions,
    finely chopped
10g minced ginger
10g minced garlic
1 red chilli, finely chopped
500g pork mince
2 tbsp soy sauce
Handful of roughly chopped basil
25g bunch of coriander, chopped

In a swift 25 minutes, you'll create a meal that's bursting with the bold flavours of ginger, garlic and chilli, all perfectly balanced with the hearty, savoury taste of pork mince. The aubergine adds a lovely, soft texture that contrasts beautifully with the fresh crunch of little gem lettuce leaves. Finished with a squeeze of lime, each bite is a high-protein, low-carb delight that's light on the tummy but heavy on satisfaction. It's an ideal choice for a healthy, flavour-packed dinner that's both speedy and splendidly tasty.

Heat the oil in a frying pan and cook the aubergine until golden and starting to soften –this will take about 10 minutes. Stir in the spring onions, ginger, garlic and chilli and cook for a further minute.

Add the pork mince to the pan and stir-fry everything together for about 5–7 minutes until browned and cooked through. Stir in the soy sauce, basil and coriander. Serve with little gem lettuce leaves and lime wedges.

NUTRITIONAL INFO PER SERVING:
254 CALORIES
28g PROTEIN
4g CARBS
14g FAT

Food Diary Barcode:

Pork Pibil Rice Bowl with Beetroot & Mixed Seed Slaw

PREP TIME: 15 MINS
COOK TIME: 2½ HRS
SERVES: 4

1kg piece of pork loin
1 onion, quartered
4 garlic cloves, peeled
   but left whole
1 tbsp cumin seeds
1 tbsp fennel seeds
2 tbsp smoked paprika
2 tsp dried oregano
1 tbsp tomato purée
1 red chilli, deseeded
400ml fresh orange juice
Sea salt and black pepper

For the slaw
200g beetroot, washed
   and topped and tailed
3 medium carrots, washed
   and topped and tailed
200g celeriac, peeled
15g fresh coriander, chopped
1 gherkin/pickled cucumber,
   chopped into small cubes
3 tbsp mixed seeds, toasted
100g pomegranate seeds
Juice of 1 lemon
2 tbsp Dijon mustard
3 tbsp extra virgin olive oil

This meal is perfect for when you have a little more time to indulge in cooking. The pork, bathed in a spiced marinade and slow-roasted to tender perfection, pulls apart effortlessly. The slaw adds a crisp, refreshing contrast to the rich pork, with the pomegranate seeds providing bursts of sweetness.

Remove all the fat from the pork loin. Place the onion, garlic, cumin and fennel seeds, paprika, oregano, tomato purée, chilli, orange juice and a teaspoon of salt and some pepper in a food processor and blitz to a paste.

Place the pork loin in a roasting tin. Pour the paste over the pork, making sure all the pork is covered and submerged in the paste. Cover with foil and leave to marinate for at least 1–2 hours, ideally overnight.

When you are ready to cook, preheat the oven to 120°C (100°C fan)/250°F/gas 1. Place the pork loin in the oven and cook for 1½ hours, or until falling apart.

Prepare the coleslaw by shredding the beetroot, carrots and celeriac through the shredding attachment in a food processor, or simply by grating on a coarse grater. Toss all the vegetables together in a bowl and add the coriander, chopped gherkin, mixed seeds and pomegranate seeds, mixing well.

Whisk the lemon juice, mustard and oil together, then pour over the vegetables and season with a pinch of salt and pepper to taste. Toss well.

Shred the pork and toss with the juices in the roasting tin. Serve with the slaw, and some rice, flatbreads and Greek-style yoghurt as well if you like.

NUTRITIONAL INFO PER SERVING:
491 CALORIES
53g PROTEIN
27g CARBS
19g FAT

Food Diary Barcode:

Pea & Ham Soup

PREP TIME: 15 MINS
COOK TIME: 25 MINS
SERVES: 7

1 tbsp olive oil
2 rashers of smoked bacon
   (fat removed), chopped
2 onions, finely chopped
1 leek, cleaned and thinly sliced
2 large carrots, peeled and diced
300g green peas
1.2 litres ham stock
300g cooked, shredded ham hock
   (smoked, if preferred)
1 bay leaf
1 tsp dried thyme or a few sprigs
   of fresh thyme
Sea salt and black pepper
Fresh parsley or chives, chopped,
   to garnish

This pea and ham soup is perfect for a chilly day or when you're in need of a fulfilling meal that feels like a warm cuddle from the inside. If you don't have ham or ham stock, this recipe would also be delicious using leftover roast chicken and chicken stock instead.

Heat the olive oil in a large saucepan, add the smoked bacon, onions, leek and carrots and fry over a medium heat until softened, stirring constantly.

Add the peas, stock, ham, bay leaf and thyme and bring to the boil, then reduce the heat and allow to simmer for 15 minutes.

Remove the bay leaf and thyme sprigs (if you've used fresh thyme). Season the soup with salt and pepper to taste. Blend until smooth, then ladle the soup into bowls. Garnish with freshly chopped parsley or chives and serve with some fresh bread, if liked.

NUTRITIONAL INFO PER SERVING:
184 CALORIES
18g PROTEIN
10g CARBS
8g FAT

Food Diary Barcode:

387
CALORIES
per serving

Slow Cooker Cashew Pork

PREP TIME: 15 MINS
COOK TIME: 5 HRS
SERVES: 6

1kg pork loin, cubed
2 tbsp apple cider vinegar
5g minced garlic
5g minced ginger
50ml reduced-salt soy sauce
3 tbsp tomato ketchup
2 tbsp cornflour
1 tsp chilli flakes
1 tbsp honey
½ tsp black pepper
80g cashews

This recipe is all about rich flavours and tender textures – imagine melt-in-your-mouth pork combined with the velvety richness of cashews, all infused with a blend of aromatic spices and seasonings. It's the perfect dish for those who crave deep, delicious flavours without spending hours in the kitchen, because the slow cooker does all the legwork.

Add everything to the slow cooker, apart from the cashews, and mix through.

Cover with a lid and cook on low for 4–5 hours.

One hour before the end of cooking time, add the cashews to the slow cooker, re-cover and cook for the final hour.

NUTRITIONAL INFO PER SERVING:
387 CALORIES
45g PROTEIN
18g CARBS
15g FAT

Food Diary Barcode:

Scan here for the
recipe video

332
CALORIES
per serving

Air Fryer Double Pork Meatballs in Tomato & Basil Sauce

PREP TIME: 15 MINS
COOK TIME: 20 MINS
SERVES: 4

1 tsp olive oil
1 small onion, very finely chopped
50g bacon medallions,
   finely chopped
10g minced garlic
500g pork mince (5% fat)
1 egg
70g breadcrumbs
1 tsp dried oregano
Salt and pepper

For the sauce
1 tsp olive oil
1 onion, finely chopped
10g minced garlic
1 x 400g tin of chopped tomatoes
250ml chicken stock
1 tsp balsamic vinegar
Large handful of basil leaves

Imagine this: succulent meatballs made with a double dose of pork, air-fried to perfection, and then smothered in a vibrant, homemade tomato and basil sauce. Sounds amazing, doesn't it? This dish is not only a feast for the taste buds but also a cinch to make.

First make the meatballs. Heat the olive oil in a frying pan over a medium heat, add the onion and bacon and fry for about 5 minutes until the onion starts to turn brown and the bacon crisps up.

Add the garlic and fry for a further 30 seconds, then tip the contents of the pan on to a plate or chopping board and allow to cool down.

Once cool, add it to a bowl with the pork mince, egg, breadcrumbs, oregano, salt and pepper. Get your hands in to combine everything and form into 16 meatballs.

There are two ways to cook the meatballs. The best (and quickest) way is to pop them into an air fryer for 12–14 minutes at 190ºC, turning them over midway through, but if you don't have an air fryer you can pan-fry them in a little olive oil until browned all over and cooked through, about 15–20 minutes.

While the meatballs are in the air fryer, get to work on your sauce.

Heat the olive oil in a large frying pan and fry the onion for about 5 minutes over a medium heat. Add the garlic and fry for 30 seconds more before adding the chopped tomatoes, chicken stock and balsamic vinegar

Cook for about 10 minutes, keeping the heat quite high to allow for everything to reduce quickly. Season with salt and pepper and stir through the basil leaves.

Once the meatballs are cooked, mix them through the sauce and serve with some pasta, if liked.

NUTRITIONAL INFO PER SERVING:
332 CALORIES
37g PROTEIN
19g CARBS
12g FAT

Food Diary Barcode:

Scan here for the recipe video

Spanish Pork & Rice

PREP TIME: 10 MINS
COOK TIME: 45 MINS
SERVES: 5

1 tbsp olive oil
500g pork fillet or loin, diced
100g reduced-fat chorizo,
  chopped
1 red onion, chopped
1 red pepper, chopped
10g minced garlic
1 tsp smoked paprika
1 tsp dried oregano
1 tsp chopped rosemary leaves
200ml red wine
300g paella or risotto rice
1 x 400g tin of chopped tomatoes
900ml chicken or vegetable stock
Chopped fresh parsley, to garnish

We're off to the sunny Mediterranean with a fantastic Spanish rice recipe that's sure to leave your taste buds dancing the flamenco! This one-pot pork, chorizo and rice dish is ideal for an easy midweek dinner, packs a real flavour punch and is certain to be a hit with the whole family.

Add the olive oil to a large frying pan over a high heat and fry the pork for 5 minutes, or until it's golden on all sides. Remove from the pan and set aside.

Reduce the heat to medium, add the chorizo, onion and pepper and fry for a couple of minutes, then add the garlic, paprika, oregano and rosemary and fry for a further 30 seconds.

Add the wine and let it bubble until reduced by about a third, then return the pork to the pan along with the rice, chopped tomatoes and stock.

Mix everything through, reduce the heat to medium-low and simmer for about 30–35 minutes, stirring often, until the rice is tender and most of the liquid has been absorbed. You may need to add some water and simmer for a bit longer if the rice isn't cooked through after 30 minutes. Serve scattered with some fresh parsley.

NUTRITIONAL INFO PER SERVING:
497 CALORIES
31g PROTEIN
63g CARBS
13g FAT

Food Diary Barcode:

Scan here for the
recipe video

2

POULTRY

289
CALORIES
per serving

Spiced Greek Chicken

PREP TIME: 10 MINS
COOK TIME: 20 MINS
SERVES: 4

1 tbsp olive oil
1 onion, chopped
1 red pepper, chopped
5g minced garlic
600g chicken breast, cubed
1½ tsp ground coriander
1½ tsp ground cumin
1 tsp ground cinnamon
300ml chicken stock
1 x 400g tin of chopped tomatoes
Handful of pitted green olives
Salt and pepper

This recipe is going to whisk you away to the sun-kissed shores of the Mediterranean. With aromatic spices like coriander, cumin and a hint of cinnamon, this dish promises a burst of flavour and flashbacks to your summer holiday with every single bite.

Heat the olive oil in a non-stick frying pan over a medium-high heat.

Add the onion, pepper and garlic and cook until the onion and pepper are soft, about 5 minutes. Add the chicken and spices and cook for a further minute.

Add the chicken stock and chopped tomatoes and season with salt and pepper. Reduce the heat and simmer for 10–15 minutes, or until the sauce is thick and the chicken is cooked through (if it starts to dry out too much, you can add a splash of water as needed).

Scatter over the green olives and serve with steamed spinach.

NUTRITIONAL INFO PER SERVING:
289 CALORIES
40g PROTEIN
12g CARBS
9g FAT

Food Diary Barcode:

Scan here for the
recipe video

Crispy Air Fryer Chicken Burgers with Cajun Mayo

PREP TIME: 20 MINS
COOK TIME: 15 MINS
SERVES: 4

For the crispy chicken

600g boneless, skinless chicken
    breasts
80g panko breadcrumbs
½ tsp salt
½ tsp black pepper
1 tsp smoked paprika
1 tsp garlic powder
1 tsp onion powder
1 tsp dried thyme
2 tsp cornflour
2 large eggs, beaten
Spray oil

For the Cajun mayo

130ml low-fat mayonnaise
½ tsp Cajun seasoning
1 tsp lemon juice

To serve

4 burger buns
1 ripe avocado, thinly sliced
1 small red onion, thinly sliced
Handful of coriander leaves

NUTRITIONAL INFO PER SERVING:
743 CALORIES
63g PROTEIN
71g CARBS
23g FAT

Food Diary Barcode:

These beauties are cooked in an air fryer for that irresistible crunch. Layered with velvety avocado, red onion and a zesty low-fat Cajun mayo that packs a punch, each burger is a carnival of flavours, topped with a sprinkle of coriander for a fresh finish. If you're in the mood for a lighter take on a fast-food favourite, these burgers are sure to tickle your fancy.

First make the Cajun mayo: mix together the low-fat mayonnaise, Cajun seasoning and lemon juice in a small bowl. Cover and refrigerate until ready to use.

Cut the chicken breasts into 1cm thick chicken steaks/burgers.

Mix the panko breadcrumbs in a bowl with the salt, black pepper, smoked paprika, garlic powder, onion powder and dried thyme.

Set up a breading station with three shallow bowls: one with the cornflour, one with the beaten eggs, and one with the panko breadcrumbs. Dredge each chicken piece in the flour (make sure to shake off any excess), then dip in the egg and finally coat with the panko breadcrumbs.

Preheat your air fryer to 200ºC. Spray the basket with a little bit of oil to prevent sticking.

Arrange the breaded chicken in the air fryer basket. Make sure not to overcrowd the basket: cook in batches if necessary. Cook for 14–16 minutes, flipping halfway through, until the chicken is golden brown and cooked through (the internal temperature should reach 75ºC).

To assemble the burgers, toast the burger buns, if you like. Spread a generous amount of the Cajun mayo on both halves of each bun. On the bottom half, place a few slices of avocado, followed by a piece of crispy chicken. Add a few slices of red onion and a sprinkle of coriander leaves. Top with the other half of the bun. Serve immediately.

426
CALORIES
per serving

Doro Wat

PREP TIME: 10 MINS,
PLUS MARINATING
COOK TIME: 45 MINS
SERVES: 4

600g chicken breast, cut into bite-sized pieces
Juice of 1 lemon
2 tbsp Berbere or Baharat spice mix (you can find the latter in most supermarkets)
1 tbsp unsalted butter
1 tsp oil
2 large onions, finely chopped
15g minced garlic
5g minced ginger
2 tbsp tomato purée
800ml chicken stock
1 tsp salt (or to taste)
4 hard-boiled eggs, peeled
Chopped parsley, to garnish

This Ethiopian chicken stew is a harmonious blend of tender chicken marinated in lemon juice and aromatic spices, simmered slowly in a sauce rich with onions, garlic and ginger. The Berbere spice mix, with its layers of heat and flavour, is the heart of this comforting stew. Topped with boiled eggs, it's a meal that's both simple and complex, best enjoyed with rice or your favourite flatbread.

In a bowl, combine the chicken pieces with the lemon juice and ½ tablespoon of the spice mix. Let it marinate for at least 30 minutes.

Add the butter and oil to a large pot or casserole and place over a high heat. Add the chicken and brown for a few minutes on each side. Remove from the pan and set aside.

Turn the heat down to medium-high, add the finely chopped onions and sauté until translucent and softened, about 5–6 minutes.

Stir in the minced garlic and ginger, the remaining spice mix and tomato purée and continue to sauté for a further minute.

Return the chicken to the pan along with the stock, cover and simmer for 15 minutes, then remove the lid and simmer for a further 15 minutes to allow the sauce to thicken. Season to taste with salt, then add the peeled hard-boiled eggs, scatter over the parsley and serve with rice, if liked.

TIP

Berbere spice mix can be quite spicy. Adjust the amount you use based on your heat preference. If you're unable to find it in shops, you can make your own mix using a combination of spices like dried chillies, paprika, fenugreek, ginger, cardamom, cinnamon and cloves.

NUTRITIONAL INFO PER SERVING:
426 CALORIES
55g PROTEIN
11g CARBS
18g FAT

Food Diary Barcode:

Honey Sesame Chicken

PREP TIME: 15 MINS,
    PLUS MARINATING
COOK TIME: 20 MINUTES
SERVES: 4

For the chicken
1 tbsp reduced-salt soy sauce
1 tbsp mirin
2 tbsp sesame oil
5g minced garlic
5g minced ginger
600g chicken breasts, sliced

For the sauce
60g honey
20ml reduced-salt soy sauce
40g reduced-sugar ketchup
15ml apple cider vinegar
5g minced garlic
5g minced ginger
30ml water

For the vegetable stir-fried rice
200g white rice (uncooked weight)
1 tbsp sesame oil
1 small onion, finely chopped
150g frozen mixed vegetables,
    defrosted
1 egg, lightly beaten
1 tbsp reduced-salt soy sauce
2 spring onions, chopped,
    to garnish
Sesame seeds, to garnish

NUTRITIONAL INFO PER SERVING:
630 CALORIES
53g PROTEIN
64g CARBS
18g FAT

Food Diary Barcode:

Here's a cracking 'fakeaway' recipe, just for you. Lean chicken is simmered in a homemade honey sauce, giving it a glossy, sticky finish that's utterly yummy. Paired with a colourful vegetable stir-fried rice, this meal is a celebration of fresh ingredients and bold tastes – and it takes hardly any time to prep and cook.

The day before, cook the rice, allow to cool and then keep in the fridge. It needs to dry out overnight before frying, as if you use freshly cooked rice for fried rice it will just clump together and be mushy.

In a bowl, combine the soy sauce, mirin, sesame oil, garlic and ginger. Add the chicken pieces, ensuring they're well coated in the marinade. Allow them to marinate for at least 15 minutes. While the chicken is marinating, mix together all of the sauce ingredients and set aside.

Heat a wok or large pan over a high heat. Cook the marinated chicken until it is cooked through, about 5–7 minutes. Stir in the sauce and cook until it reduces and the chicken is coated in a thick sauce. Set aside and keep warm.

For the stir-fried rice, heat the sesame oil in a wok or large frying pan over a medium-high heat. Add the onion and cook until it is translucent. Add the mixed vegetables, stirring frequently until they are heated through.

Push the vegetables to the side of the pan, add the egg and stir until it scrambles. Once cooked, stir the vegetables through the eggs.

Add the chilled rice to the pan, breaking up any clumps. Add the soy sauce and stir-fry for 3–4 minutes until everything is well combined.

To serve, place a portion of the vegetable stir-fried rice on a plate, top with the sticky honey sesame chicken and garnish with chopped spring onions and sesame seeds.

356
CALORIES
per serving

Simple Mole

PREP TIME: 10 MINS
COOK TIME: 30 MINS
SERVES: 6

1 tsp olive oil
900g chicken breasts
Chopped coriander leaves,
   to garnish

For the mole sauce
1 tsp oil
1 onion, chopped
10g minced garlic
1 tbsp chipotle paste
½ tsp ground cinnamon
½ tsp ground cumin
150g tomatoes, diced
50g almond butter or
   peanut butter
40g raisins
1 tbsp unsweetened
   cocoa powder
500ml chicken stock
1 tbsp honey (or to taste)
Sea salt

Mole (pronounced 'mo-lay') is unique, to say the least, combining the unlikely duo of chilli and chocolate to create a rich, thick concoction that's a staple in Mexican cooking. It's a distinctive taste that may not be for everyone, but its rich tapestry of flavours is a celebration of Mexican ingredients.

Start by making the mole sauce. Heat the olive oil in a saucepan, then add the onion and sauté until it is translucent. Stir in the garlic, chipotle paste, cinnamon and cumin and cook for another minute.

Add the tomatoes, almond or peanut butter, raisins, cocoa powder, chicken stock and honey and bring to a simmer. Let the sauce simmer for about 10 minutes to thicken slightly, then blitz in a blender until very smooth.

Pour the sauce back into the pan. Season to taste with salt and a little extra honey if you want it sweeter.

While the sauce is simmering, pan-fry the chicken. To do this, heat another 1 teaspoon of oil in a separate frying pan, add the chicken breasts and pan-fry until cooked through.

Serve the chicken, spoon some of the mole on top (a little goes a long way, as it's very rich) and garnish with some chopped coriander leaves. You could serve this with some rice and black beans, and a pineapple salsa, if liked.

NUTRITIONAL INFO PER SERVING:
356 CALORIES
49g PROTEIN
13g CARBS
12g FAT

Food Diary Barcode:

494
CALORIES
per serving

Nasi Goreng

PREP TIME: 10 MINS
COOK TIME: 20 MINS
SERVES: 4

1 tbsp coconut oil
500g chicken breast,
   finely chopped
10g minced ginger
10g minced garlic
1 small onion, finely chopped
1 red chilli, sliced
3 eggs
250g (dried weight) basmati
   rice, cooked then chilled
   (*see* Note)
1 tbsp fish sauce
3 tbsp kecap manis (or use
   2 tbsp dark soy sauce
   and 1 tbsp honey)

**Otherwise known as Indonesian chicken fried rice, this is
so popular you can even order it for breakfast in Bali! It's
absolutely my favourite chicken fried rice recipe; hopefully
once you've made it, it will become yours too.**

Heat the coconut oil in a wok over a very high heat until it begins
to smoke, then add the chicken and fry until golden brown.

Move the chicken to the edge of the wok, then add the ginger,
garlic, onion and chilli and lightly fry for a minute. Add the eggs
and let them sit for 30 seconds or so, without moving them.
Partially mix the eggs, then let them set again and repeat this
a few times until they're cooked through. (If you just mix them
straight into the mixture they won't cook properly and will go
all weird.)

Add the chilled, cooked rice, fish sauce and the kecap manis.
Fry, mixing continuously for 2–3 minutes, until everything is
heated through.

Serve in bowls with a fried egg on top and scattered with sliced
cucumber and spring onions.

> **NOTE**
>
> Using cold rice is essential
> when doing any fried rice dish,
> as freshly cooked rice is soft
> and watery and won't produce
> the right results. Rice you've
> cooked the day before and
> chilled in the fridge is dryer and
> harder and MUCH better for
> fried rice dishes. If you forget to
> do this the day before, at least
> chill your rice with cold water
> as soon as you've cooked it so
> you're not putting hot rice into
> the pan.

NUTRITIONAL INFO PER SERVING:
494 CALORIES
38g PROTEIN
63g CARBS
10g FAT

Food Diary Barcode:

Scan here for the
recipe video

303
CALORIES
per serving

Slow Cooker Butter Chicken

PREP TIME: 15 MINS
COOK TIME: 4 HRS
SERVES: 5

30g butter
2 onions, sliced
20g minced garlic
20g minced ginger
1 tsp garam masala
2 tsp curry powder
60g tomato purée
1kg chicken breast, cubed
100ml water
1 tsp salt
1 tbsp cornflour
150g low-fat natural yoghurt

With a traditional butter chicken recipe, it is absolutely delightful to dive into that creamy, buttery goodness, but it's often a no-go for people who are trying to eat more healthily. This lower-fat slow cooker version is simply delicious but with a fraction of the calories.

Heat the butter in a frying pan over a low-medium heat and gently fry the onions for 10 minutes until soft but not coloured.

Add the garlic, ginger, garam masala, curry powder and tomato purée to the onions and fry for a minute more, then tip into the slow cooker with all of the other ingredients except the yoghurt.

Cover with the lid and cook on medium for 4 hours.

At the end of cooking, stir through the yoghurt and serve with naan or rice, if liked.

NUTRITIONAL INFO PER SERVING:
303 CALORIES
50g PROTEIN
10g CARBS
7g FAT

Food Diary Barcode:

Scan here for the
recipe video

475 CALORIES *per serving*

Spiced Chicken with Creamy Coconut Sauce

PREP TIME: 15 MINS, PLUS MARINATING
COOK TIME: 30 MINS
SERVES: 4

2 tbsp olive oil
1 tsp ground allspice or mixed spice
1 tsp dried thyme
½ tsp cayenne pepper (adjust for heat)
1 tsp garlic powder
½ tsp salt
Good few grinds of black pepper
1 tbsp lime juice
600g chicken breasts, sliced into steaks

For the creamy coconut sauce
1 onion, finely chopped
5g minced garlic
5g minced ginger
1 chilli pepper, finely chopped (deseeded for less heat)
1 x 400ml tin of coconut milk
¼ tsp salt
1 tbsp lime juice
1 tsp paprika
Sea salt and black pepper

This was a classic example of how I come up with a recipe. I was in Manchester shooting the photos for this recipe book and we went to a Caribbean restaurant one evening for dinner. The publisher, Lauren, ordered a dish that was something like what you're about to make. It looked delicious and this is my take on it.

In a bowl, mix the olive oil, allspice or mixed spice, thyme, cayenne pepper, garlic powder, salt, pepper and lime juice. Coat the chicken breasts evenly with this marinade. Let them marinate for at least 30 minutes, ideally overnight.

When you're ready to cook, place a frying pan over a medium-high heat and add the chicken breasts. Cook until they get a nice colour on them and are almost cooked through, about 5–10 minutes. Remove from the pan and set aside.

Add the onion to the same pan and fry until it's softened. Add the garlic, ginger and chilli and fry for a further minute. Add the coconut milk, salt, lime juice, paprika and season with salt and pepper. Add the chicken back to the pan and reduce the heat to a simmer.

Simmer for about 10 minutes until the sauce has thickened and the chicken has fully cooked through.

Serve with chopped coriander, lime wedges and rice, if liked.

NUTRITIONAL INFO PER SERVING:
475 CALORIES
48g PROTEIN
10g CARBS
27g FAT

Food Diary Barcode:

249
CALORIES
per serving

Zingy Crispy Glazed Chicken

PREP TIME: 15 MINS
COOK TIME: 30 MINS
SERVES: 4

500g chicken breast fillets
1 egg, beaten
50g breadcrumbs or crushed
    cornflakes
4 tbsp lemon juice
2 tbsp water
2 tbsp Worcestershire sauce
2 tsp olive oil
30g honey
½ tsp chilli flakes
½ tsp mixed herbs

This recipe is outrageously delicious, taking the ordinary and making it extraordinary. If you think chicken breast is bland, think again – the crunchy breadcrumbs envelop a juicy chicken breast, which is then smothered in a rich, tangy and sweet glaze. Give this recipe a go and your taste buds will thank you!

Preheat the oven to 200ºC (180ºC fan)/400ºF/gas 6 and lightly grease a baking tray.

Slice the chicken breasts in half to create thin chicken steaks (this makes them much easier to cook).

Put the beaten egg in one shallow bowl and the breadcrumbs or crushed cornflakes in another. Dip the chicken into the egg then into the breadcrumbs or cornflakes, pressing them gently to coat. Place the crumbed chicken on the greased tray and bake in the oven for 25 minutes. Once the chicken is ready, remove from the oven and set aside.

While the chicken is in the oven make the glaze: add all the remaining ingredients to a bowl and whisk to combine.

Place a large frying pan over a medium heat and add the glaze mixture from the bowl. Simmer for a few minutes, stirring constantly until the glaze thickens. Add the cooked chicken breasts to the frying pan, spoon over the glaze and serve.

NUTRITIONAL INFO PER SERVING:
249 CALORIES
30g PROTEIN
20g CARBS
5g FAT

Food Diary Barcode:

Scan here for the
recipe video

Chicken Gyros

**PREP TIME: 15 MINS,
    PLUS MARINATING
COOK TIME: 20 MINS
SERVES: 4**

3 tbsp olive oil, plus 1 tbsp
    for frying
2 tbsp lemon juice
10g minced garlic
1 tsp dried oregano
½ tsp smoked paprika
½ tsp ground cumin
½ tsp salt
600g chicken breast,
    cut into thin strips

For the tzatziki
200g Greek yoghurt
1 medium cucumber, deseeded
    and finely grated
5g minced garlic
1 tbsp chopped fresh dill
1 tbsp lemon juice
Sea salt and black pepper

To serve
4 pitta breads
Chopped lettuce
Sliced tomato
Thinly sliced red onion

Marinated chicken strips, bursting with lemony zest and a medley of spices, nestle snugly in warm pitta bread, accompanied by the crunch of fresh veggies. But the real pièce de résistance is the homemade tzatziki, a creamy, garlicky sauce with a refreshing cucumber twist. It's a doddle to whip up for a casual lunch or a dinner that'll have everyone wrapped up in the joy of simple, flavourful Greek cooking.

In a large bowl, combine the 3 tablespoons olive oil, lemon juice, minced garlic, dried oregano, smoked paprika, cumin and salt.

Add the chicken strips and toss well to coat. Cover the bowl and marinate in the fridge for at least 2 hours.

While the chicken is marinating, prepare the tzatziki. In a bowl, combine the Greek yoghurt, grated cucumber, minced garlic, chopped dill and lemon juice and season with salt and pepper. Mix well and refrigerate until ready to serve.

Heat the tablespoon of oil in a large frying pan over a medium heat. Add the marinated chicken strips and cook for 5–7 minutes on each side, or until the chicken is cooked through and golden brown.

Assemble the gyros. Warm the pitta breads briefly in the oven or toaster. Top each pitta bread with some lettuce, tomato and red onion. Add the cooked chicken strips and top with a generous amount of tzatziki.

Roll up the pitta breads tightly, wrapping the bottom half in foil if desired to keep everything together. Serve immediately.

NUTRITIONAL INFO PER SERVING:
566 CALORIES
59g PROTEIN
33g CARBS
22g FAT

Food Diary Barcode:

Chicken Katsu Curry

PREP TIME: 20 MINS
COOK TIME: 20 MINS
SERVES: 4

For the chicken katsu
600g chicken breasts
50g plain flour
1 egg, beaten
100g panko breadcrumbs
Sea salt and black pepper
Olive oil spray

For the curry sauce
1 tsp coconut oil
1 large onion, finely chopped
1 large carrot, peeled
   and chopped
7g minced garlic
7g minced ginger
2 tbsp curry powder
1 tbsp plain flour
500ml chicken stock
2 tsp soy sauce
1 tsp honey
1 bay leaf

This dish delivers all the crispy satisfaction and rich flavour of a katsu curry without the heaviness. Lean chicken breasts, transformed into golden-brown katsu through the magic of the air fryer, are the stars of this dish. The silky-smooth curry sauce, rich with the warmth of spices, tender veggies and a hint of sweetness from honey, is a perfect match for the chicken. It's a nourishing spin on the beloved Japanese classic.

Cut the chicken breasts into thin steaks, about 1cm thick. Season with salt and pepper. Set up three shallow dishes: one with flour, one with beaten egg and one with panko breadcrumbs.

Dip each chicken piece first in flour, shaking off any excess, then in egg, and finally coat thoroughly in breadcrumbs. Place the breaded chicken on a plate. Set aside.

To make the sauce, heat the coconut oil in a large saucepan over a medium heat. Add the onion and carrot and fry until softened. Add the garlic and ginger and continue to cook for another 30 seconds.

Stir the curry powder and flour into the vegetable mixture and cook for a minute. Gradually add the chicken stock, stirring constantly to prevent any lumps. Add the soy sauce, honey and bay leaf. Bring the sauce to a simmer and let it cook for about 15 minutes until the vegetables are tender and the sauce has thickened.

While the sauce is simmering, heat your air fryer to 180°C. Spray the chicken pieces lightly with olive oil and place them in the air fryer (depending on the size of your air fryer, you might need to cook in batches). Cook for 15–20 minutes, or until the chicken is golden brown and has an internal temperature of 74°C.

When the sauce has simmered for 15 minutes, blitz with a hand blender, then simmer for a further 5 minutes.

Once the chicken is done, slice it into strips. Serve the chicken over rice, with a generous amount of curry sauce poured over the top.

NUTRITIONAL INFO PER SERVING:
470 CALORIES
55g PROTEIN
40g CARBS
10g FAT

Food Diary Barcode:

315
CALORIES
per serving

Diet Coke Chicken

PREP TIME: 10 MINS
COOK TIME: 20 MINS
SERVES: 3

500g chicken breast, chopped
1 tsp garlic powder
1 tsp onion powder
½ tsp paprika
330ml Diet Coke
100g tomato ketchup
2 tbsp reduced-salt soy sauce
1 tbsp rice vinegar
½ tsp chilli powder
1 tsp olive oil
Spring onions, chopped,
   to garnish

Diet Coke chicken is a game-changer, a rule-breaker; it's sweet, it's tangy, it's a little bit quirky, and it's absolutely delicious. If you're thinking 'Diet Coke . . . in chicken? You're having a laugh, mate!', trust me, once you've tried it, you'll be hooked, my friend.

In a bowl combine the chicken with ½ teaspoon of the garlic powder, ½ teaspoon of the onion powder and the paprika. Set aside.

In a jug mix the Diet Coke, ketchup, soy sauce, rice vinegar, chilli powder and the remaining garlic powder and onion powder.

Heat the oil in a frying pan over a high heat and add the chicken. Pan-fry for 5–7 minutes until it starts to turn golden brown – it doesn't need to be fully cooked through at this stage.

Keeping the heat on high, pour in the contents of the jug. Simmer for about 10 minutes until the sauce has really thickened and is coating the chicken. Serve with chopped spring onions scattered over the top.

NUTRITIONAL INFO PER SERVING:
315 CALORIES
51g PROTEIN
12g CARBS
7g FAT

Food Diary Barcode:

Scan here for the
recipe video

Less Faff Coq au Vin

PREP TIME: 15 MINS
COOK TIME: 1 HR 15 MINS
SERVES: 4

600g chicken thigh fillets
20g butter
200g diced smoked bacon,
    fat removed
12–15 shallots, peeled but
    left whole
250g mushrooms, quartered
15g minced garlic
2 tbsp plain flour
500ml red wine
Few sprigs of fresh thyme
    (or 1 tsp dried)
Few sprigs of fresh rosemary
    (or 1 tsp dried)
1 tbsp tomato purée
750ml chicken stock
Sea salt and black pepper
Fresh parsley, chopped,
    for garnish

Unveil the rustic charm of French cooking with my simplified take on the classic that doesn't skimp on taste. This dish is a delightful medley of tender chicken thigh fillets, smoky bacon and earthy mushrooms, all bathed in a rich red wine sauce. It's a fuss-free recipe that promises a hearty meal with a depth of flavour that normally comes from hours of slaving away. Serve it up with a side of crusty bread or fluffy potatoes, and let each spoonful transport you to the serene French countryside. Bon appétit!

Season the chicken pieces all over with pepper. Melt the butter in a large casserole or heavy-based pan over a high heat. Add the chicken pieces and brown on all sides, then remove and set aside.

Add the bacon to the same pan and fry until it starts crisp up, then add the shallots and mushrooms and continue to cook until they take on some colour. Add the minced garlic and cook for another minute. Sprinkle the flour over the mixture and stir well, cooking for another 1–2 minutes.

Pour in the red wine and keeping the heat quite high, simmer uncovered for 10 minutes to allow the alcohol to burn off and the liquid to reduce by about a third.

Add the thyme, rosemary, tomato purée and chicken stock and return the browned chicken pieces to the pan. Reduce the heat to medium and simmer uncovered for 45 minutes to about 1 hour, or until the chicken is tender and the sauce has reduced and thickened. Once done, remove the rosemary and thyme sprigs, then taste and adjust the seasoning with more salt and pepper if necessary.

Ladle the coq au vin into bowls, garnishing with freshly chopped parsley. Serve with crusty bread or potatoes on the side to mop up the delicious sauce.

For an even richer flavour, marinate the chicken pieces in the wine overnight with some sliced onions and carrots. Drain and use the wine in the recipe, discarding the vegetables.

NUTRITIONAL INFO PER SERVING:
424 CALORIES
50g PROTEIN
11g CARBS
20g FAT

Food Diary Barcode:

486
CALORIES
per serving

Chicken, Bean & Pasta Soup with Walnut Pesto

PREP TIME: 25 MINS
COOK TIME: 50 MINS
SERVES: 6

For the stock
6 skinless chicken thighs
2 large carrots, chopped
2 stalks celery
1 onion, halved
4 garlic cloves, peeled but
    left whole
Small bunch of flat-leaf parsley
Sea salt

For the soup
1 tbsp olive oil
1 small onion, finely chopped
10g minced garlic
1 large leek, chopped
2 medium potatoes, peeled
    and diced
1 large carrot, peeled and diced
1 sprig of rosemary, leaves finely
    chopped
400g tin of chopped tomatoes
75g small pasta shapes
100g savoy cabbage, finely
    shredded
400g tin of borlotti or cannellini
    beans

For the pesto
50g walnut pieces
5g garlic
Large bunch of basil
Extra virgin olive oil
4 tbsp finely grated Parmesan
    cheese

Dive into a bowl of comfort with this hearty soup, an ensemble that's perfect for warming you up on a nippy evening. The addition of walnut pesto adds a unique, nutty twist, enriching the soup with a creamy texture and a punch of flavour.

Place the chicken thighs in a large saucepan with the carrots, celery, onion, garlic and parsley. Pour over 2 litres of cold water and add a teaspoon of sea salt. Bring to a gentle simmer, then cook for 30 minutes until the chicken is very tender. Remove the chicken from the stock and shred into pieces. Strain the stock into a jug, squashing the vegetables into the stock through the sieve.

Meanwhile, heat the oil in a large saucepan, add the chopped onion and cook for 4 minutes, then stir in the garlic, leek, potatoes, carrot and rosemary and cook for another 5 minutes.

Tip in the chopped tomatoes and pour in the stock from the chicken. Bring to a simmer and cook for a further 15 minutes.

Add the pasta and cook for a further 8 minutes, then stir in the savoy cabbage and beans and simmer for 3 minutes.

To make the pesto, place the walnuts in a food processor with the garlic and blitz, then add the basil, a good pinch of salt and a glug of extra virgin olive oil. Transfer to a bowl and stir through most of the Parmesan.

Ladle the soup into bowls and serve with a dollop of walnut pesto and the remaining Parmesan sprinkled on top. Enjoy with some toasted bread, if liked.

NUTRITIONAL INFO PER SERVING:
486 CALORIES
37g PROTEIN
35g CARBS
22g FAT

Food Diary Barcode:

400
CALORIES
per serving

Chicken Tikka Masala

**PREP TIME: 10 MINS,
PLUS MARINATING
COOK TIME: 25 MINS
SERVES: 4**

1 tbsp butter
1 large onion, finely chopped
10g minced garlic
10g minced ginger
1 tbsp curry powder
1 tsp garam masala
1 tsp paprika
1 x 400g tin of chopped tomatoes
200ml coconut milk
½ tsp salt
1 tsp sugar
Small bunch of fresh coriander,
    chopped

For the chicken tikka
100ml Greek yoghurt (0% fat)
1 tbsp lemon juice
1 tbsp tandoori masala
5g minced ginger
5g minced garlic
½ tsp salt
600g chicken breasts, cut
    into bite-sized chunks

Set your table for a beloved classic from the Indian takeaway with this recipe. It's packed with stunning flavours, combining marinated, spiced chicken with a rich and creamy tomato sauce. Whether you choose the smoky charm of the barbecue for a tandoori twist or the convenience of your trusty pan, the result is a luscious curry that I think you'll love. Oh, and it's also a fraction of the calories compared to the takeaway version.

Start by marinating the chicken tikka. In a bowl, mix together all the marinade ingredients, then add the chicken and mix to make sure it's thoroughly coated. Cover and refrigerate for at least 1 hour, but overnight if possible.

To cook the chicken, you have two options: to make a tandoori-style chicken tikka masala, thread the chicken onto skewers and cook on the barbecue until cooked through and nicely charred in places. Alternatively, heat the butter in a large pan over a medium heat. Add the marinated chicken to the pan and cook for about 5–7 minutes until the chicken is lightly browned on all sides. Remove and set aside.

Add the onion to the pan and cook until softened and starting to brown (about 5–7 minutes). Add the garlic and ginger to the pan, stir and cook for another minute until fragrant. Stir in the curry powder, garam masala and paprika and cook for another minute until the spices are well combined with the onions.

Add the chopped tomatoes, coconut milk, salt and sugar. Stir until everything is well combined, then reduce the heat to medium, cover the pan and let it simmer for about 15 minutes. After 15 minutes, uncover the pan and add the cooked chicken. If the sauce is too thick, you can add a bit more coconut milk to thin it; if it's too thin, let it simmer uncovered for another 5–10 minutes.

Stir in the chopped coriander just before serving with rice and naan, if liked.

NUTRITIONAL INFO PER SERVING:
400 CALORIES
51g PROTEIN
13g CARBS
16g FAT

Food Diary Barcode:

581
CALORIES
per serving

Creamy Chicken Pot Pie with a Crisp Corn Crust

PREP TIME: 20 MINS
COOK TIME: 1 HR
SERVES: 6

2 tbsp olive oil
1 large leek, thinly sliced
1 onion, finely chopped
10g minced garlic
400g chicken thighs, cut
   into bite-sized pieces
300ml low-fat crème fraîche
300ml chicken stock
1 tbsp Dijon mustard
2 tbsp flat-leaf parsley, chopped
Sea salt and black pepper

For the corn topping
125g plain flour
½ tsp baking powder
125g polenta
110g butter, melted
2 large free-range eggs, beaten
250ml buttermilk
100g low-fat mature Cheddar,
   grated
75g frozen corn, defrosted

Whip up a heart-warming chicken pie topped with a delightfully crisp corn crust, perfect for those evenings when comfort food is just what the family needs. In just 20 minutes of prep time, you'll combine the savoury goodness of leeks, garlic and tender chicken thighs with a creamy, mustard-infused sauce. The pièce de résistance, a golden cornbread topping, enhanced with sweetcorn kernels and mature Cheddar, transforms this from a simple pie to a showstopping centrepiece. Ready in an hour, it's not just tasty but packed with protein, ideal for keeping everyone satisfied and full of energy.

Preheat the oven to 180ºC (160ºC fan)/350ºF/gas 4. Heat the olive oil in a frying pan and cook the leek and onion over a low-medium heat for 7–8 minutes until really softened. Stir in the garlic and then the chicken pieces and cook until the chicken is browned all over. Stir in the crème fraîche, stock and Dijon mustard and simmer for 10 minutes until the sauce is slightly thickened. Season to taste with a little salt and some pepper. Stir through the parsley and transfer to a 2-litre pie dish.

To make the topping, put the plain flour, baking powder and polenta into a bowl and mix together well. In a jug, mix together the butter, eggs and buttermilk until well combined, then pour into the flour mixture and beat together well. Mix in most of the cheese and all the corn – you should now have a thick batter mixture.

Spoon the mixture over the top of the chicken and sprinkle over the remaining cheese. Bake in the oven for 25 minutes until golden.

NUTRITIONAL INFO PER SERVING:
581 CALORIES
16g PROTEIN
27g CARBS
41g FAT

Food Diary Barcode:

477 CALORIES per serving

Chicken Enchiladas

PREP TIME: 15 MINS
COOK TIME: 40 MINS
SERVES: 4

For the sauce
1 tsp olive oil
1 onion, finely chopped
1 tsp smoked paprika
1 tsp ground cumin
½ tsp chilli powder
1 tsp dried oregano
500g passata
50g low-fat Cheddar cheese,
    grated
1 x 400g tin of black beans,
    rinsed and drained
    (250g drained weight)

For the filling
1 tsp olive oil
500g chicken breast, sliced
1 onion, sliced
2 peppers, sliced
8 lighter tortilla wraps
100g low-fat Cheddar cheese,
    grated

If you thought the chicken enchiladas you make with a few sachets from a meal kit were good, this enchilada recipe is going to blow your mind. No pre-made mixes, no packets with a 20-year shelf life, just fresh ingredients and a whole lot of flavour. But don't worry my friends, it's far quicker and easier than you think to serve up a plate of these and what's more, the whole family will love them.

Preheat the oven to 200ºC (180ºC fan)/400ºF/gas 6.

To make the sauce, heat the olive oil in a pan over a medium heat, add the onion and cook, stirring, until golden. Add the spices, oregano and passata and simmer for 8–10 minutes. Just before the end of cooking, add the 50g grated cheese and the drained beans and mix through, then set aside.

While the sauce is simmering, prepare the filling. Heat the olive oil in a frying pan over a high heat and fry the chicken until lightly browned, then remove and set aside. Add the onion and pepper slices and fry these until browned. Return the chicken to the pan along with half of the sauce mixture and stir to combine.

Evenly distribute the filling mixture between the tortilla wraps and roll up, placing each one in a baking dish as you go (they should fit snugly in a single layer). Cover with the rest of the sauce and scatter over the 100g grated cheese.

Bake in the oven for 20–25 minutes until the cheese is bubbling. Serve hot.

NUTRITIONAL INFO PER SERVING:
477 CALORIES
48g PROTEIN
42g CARBS
13g FAT

Food Diary Barcode:

Scan here for the recipe video

345
CALORIES
per serving

Chicken Dopiaza

PREP TIME: 10 MINS
COOK TIME: 20 MINS
SERVES: 3

3 tsp oil
2 onions, 1 finely chopped,
   1 cut into chunks
1 red pepper, cut into chunks
1 green pepper, cut into chunks
600g chicken breast, chopped
   into large pieces
25g minced garlic
25g minced ginger
½ tsp paprika
3 tsp curry powder
2 x 400g tins of chopped
   tomatoes
1 tsp mango chutney
1 tsp Worcestershire sauce
Large handful of fresh coriander,
   leaves and stems, chopped

Chicken dopiaza is one of the most popular curries found on takeaway menus across the country. And for good reason: it's an absolute belter of a chicken curry! Give this healthier version a whirl and save yourself a trip to the takeaway.

Place a wok or a large frying pan over a high heat and add 1 teaspoon of the oil. Once it's starting to smoke, add the onion, red pepper and green pepper chunks (reserve the finely chopped onion for later). Fry for 1–2 minutes until you start to see some charring on the peppers. Remove from the pan and set aside.

Heat another teaspoon of oil in the same pan. Once it's hot, add the chicken and fry for a few minutes until it's turning brown on the outside. (You don't need to cook it fully through at this stage, just get some nice colour on it so no pink bits are visible.) Remove from the pan and set aside.

Reduce the heat to medium-high and add the final teaspoon of oil. Add the finely chopped onion and fry for a few minutes until softened, then add the garlic and ginger and fry for a further 30 seconds. Add the paprika and curry powder and fry for a further 30 seconds.

Add the charred onions and peppers back to the pan along with the cooked chicken, chopped tomatoes, mango chutney and Worcestershire sauce. Reduce the heat to medium-low, cover and simmer for about 10 minutes.

After 10 minutes, remove the lid and add the coriander, reserving a few leaves to garnish. Simmer for a further 5 minutes with the lid off to allow the dopiaza to thicken.

Serve garnished with the reserved coriander.

NUTRITIONAL INFO PER SERVING:
345 CALORIES
49g PROTEIN
17g CARBS
9g FAT

Food Diary Barcode:

Scan here for the recipe video

Pimm's Glazed Chicken

**PREP TIME: 10 MINS,
PLUS MARINATING
COOK TIME: 20–25 MINS
SERVES: 4**

600g chicken breasts
120ml Pimm's No. 1
50g orange marmalade
½ tsp chilli flakes (adjust
   according to your heat
   preference)
½ tsp salt
Black pepper
1 tsp oil
330ml diet lemonade
Orange zest and chopped mint,
   to garnish (optional)

This dish brings the quintessential British summer drink into your main course, combining it with the tangy sweetness of orange marmalade for an innovative glaze that's simply delicious. After a quick seal, the chicken is simmered in the Pimm's and lemonade reduction, resulting in a lusciously sticky sauce. Garnish with fresh orange zest and mint to enhance the citrus notes and add a touch of brightness. It's an ideal meal to serve up when the sun is shining and the garden is calling.

Slice the chicken breasts horizontally so they're about 1–2cm thick.

Add the Pimm's, marmalade, chilli flakes, salt, and some freshly ground black pepper to a bowl and mix thoroughly (don't worry if the marmalade doesn't dissolve completely). Add the chicken to the mixture and allow it to marinate in the fridge for at least 2 hours, ideally overnight.

When you're ready to cook, heat the oil in a large frying pan over a medium-high heat. Once hot, add the chicken breasts (reserve the marinade) and sear them for about 2 minutes on each side, or until they develop a brown coating. Pour the reserved marinade over the top along with the diet lemonade. This may foam up like crazy and look a bit odd to begin with, but as it reduces the foam will dissipate.

Turn the heat up to high and simmer for 10–12 minutes, or until the sauce has significantly reduced down and is coating the chicken. The texture of the sauce should be thick, almost like ketchup.

Serve, sprinkled with fresh orange zest and some chopped mint for added freshness, if you like. This dish pairs well with a crisp green salad, roasted sweet potato wedges or steamed green beans.

NUTRITIONAL INFO PER SERVING:
274 CALORIES
45g PROTEIN
10g CARBS
6g FAT

Food Diary Barcode:

Red Pesto Stuffed Chicken Breasts Wrapped in Ham

PREP TIME: 15 MINS
COOK TIME: 35 MINS
SERVES: 4

600g chicken breasts
100g sundried tomatoes, chopped
50g mozzarella, grated
40g red pesto
4 slices of good-quality ham
Sea salt and black pepper
Basil leaves, to garnish

Filled with the tangy intensity of sundried tomatoes and the creamy, melted bliss of mozzarella, each chicken breast becomes a treasure trove of flavour. Oven-baked in their own little foil parcels, these chicken delights are succulent, brimming with flavour and promise to deliver a burst of sunshine with every bite.

Preheat the oven to 200°C (180°C fan)/400°F/gas 6.

Place each chicken breast on a chopping board. Make a deep slit along the side of each breast to create a pocket, making sure you don't cut all the way through.

Mix together the sundried tomatoes, mozzarella and pesto until combined, then spoon a quarter of this mixture into the pocket in each chicken breast. Wrap each chicken breast in a slice of ham, then place on a square of foil and loosely wrap it so that the juices are contained once it starts to cook.

Place the foil packets on a baking tray and pop into the oven for 30–35 minutes. Serve garnished with fresh basil leaves alongside some new potatoes and Tenderstem broccoli.

NUTRITIONAL INFO PER SERVING:
373 CALORIES
57g PROTEIN
7g CARBS
13g FAT

Food Diary Barcode:

309
CALORIES
per serving

Orange Chicken

PREP TIME: 5 MINS
COOK TIME: 4 HRS
SERVES: 6

1kg chicken breast, cubed
15g cornflour
100ml chicken stock
100ml orange juice
50ml soy sauce
50g honey
10g minced garlic
10g minced ginger
1 tsp chilli flakes
Pinch of black pepper
Sesame seeds and chopped
    spring onion, to garnish

This is a winner of a sweet and savoury, slow cooker fakeaway-style recipe. The chicken is beautifully juicy, the sauce is rich and sweet and tastes like it should be much unhealthier and higher in calories than it really is.

Put the chicken into a slow cooker.

Combine the cornflour, chicken stock, orange juice, soy sauce, honey, garlic, ginger, chilli flakes and black pepper in a jug, then pour over the chicken.

Add the lid and cook on low for 4 hours.

Serve scattered with the sesame seeds and spring onions.

NOTE

For a really rich, thick sauce, remove the chicken from the slow cooker at the end of the cooking time and set aside. Pour the sauce into a pan and simmer on the stovetop until it has reduced and thickened.

NUTRITIONAL INFO PER SERVING:
309 CALORIES
51g PROTEIN
15g CARBS
5g FAT

Food Diary Barcode:

Scan here for the
recipe video

583
CALORIES
per serving

Thai Red Curry Roast Chicken

PREP TIME: 20 MINS,
   PLUS MARINATING
COOK TIME: 30 MINS
SERVES: 4

1kg chicken, jointed into 8 pieces
2 tbsp Thai red curry paste
1 x 400ml tin of coconut milk
Zest of 1 lime
1 tsp fish sauce
1 tbsp honey
1 x 400g tin of chopped tomatoes
Small bunch of coriander,
   chopped
4 spring onions, chopped

Get ready to savour the vibrant tastes of Thailand and bring a twist to your roast dinner. With minimal prep and a burst of flavours, it's an ideal meal to impress your family or guests, promising a culinary escape to the bustling streets of Bangkok from the comfort of your home.

Place the chicken pieces in a roasting tin. Mix together the Thai curry paste, coconut milk, lime zest, fish sauce and honey in a jug and pour over the chicken. Cover and leave to marinate in the fridge overnight.

When you are ready to cook, preheat the oven to 180°C (160°C fan)/350°F/gas 4.

Add the chopped tomatoes to the chicken and mix everything around. Place in the oven and roast for 25 minutes until the chicken is cooked through and the sauce has thickened. Preheat the grill and cook for a further 5 minutes under the grill to brown off the chicken.

Scatter with the chopped coriander and spring onions and serve with stir-fried greens, if liked.

NUTRITIONAL INFO PER SERVING:
583 CALORIES
79g PROTEIN
15g CARBS
23g FAT

Food Diary Barcode:

Spicy Air Fryer Chicken Tenders

PREP TIME: 10 MINS
COOK TIME: 12–15 MINS
SERVES: 4

130g Dorito Chilli Heatwave Tortilla
   Chips
1 tsp garlic powder
1 tsp onion powder
1 tsp chipotle paste
1 tsp dried thyme
1 egg, beaten
600g chicken breasts, sliced into
   small fillets or 'tenders'

You'll love the fiery crunch of these chicken tenders. The air fryer works its magic, encasing the chicken in a golden, crispy, spicy armour while keeping the inside juicy and tender. Quick to prep and even quicker to disappear from the plate, these tenders are a sure-fire hit for any gathering or to give a spicy twist to your weeknight dinners. Serve them up with your favourite dipping sauce and watch them become the new staple in your culinary repertoire.

Place the tortilla chips, garlic powder, onion powder, chipotle paste and dried thyme in a food processor. Pulse until they are crushed into a texture like breadcrumbs. Tip into a shallow bowl.

One by one, dip your chicken tenders first into the beaten egg, making sure they are fully coated. Allow any excess egg to drip off. Next, roll your chicken tenders in the spicy tortilla chip mixture. Ensure they are fully coated, pressing the mixture onto the chicken if needed.

Place your breaded chicken tenders into the basket or tray of your air fryer, leaving a little space between each piece to ensure even cooking.

Cook at 200°C for 12–15 minutes, or until the chicken is cooked through (the internal temperature should be 74°C) and the coating is crispy and golden. Make sure to turn them halfway through cooking.

Serve with your favourite dipping sauce and enjoy!

NUTRITIONAL INFO PER SERVING:
419 CALORIES
49g PROTEIN
22g CARBS
15g FAT

Food Diary Barcode:

553
CALORIES
per serving

Sherry Chicken Pilaf

PREP TIME: 15 MINS
COOK TIME: 25 MINS
SERVES: 4

2 tbsp olive oil
1 onion, finely chopped
15g minced garlic
3 chicken breasts, cubed
50ml dry sherry
Pinch of saffron
600ml chicken stock
175g basmati rice
50g raisins
50g pine nuts, toasted
Zest and juice of 1 small lemon
Large bunch of flat-leaf parsley,
    roughly chopped
Sea salt and black pepper

High in protein and brimming with recovery-promoting carbohydrates, this pilaf is a balanced, satisfying meal that's sure to become a regular in your culinary repertoire.

Heat the oil in a large frying pan, add the onion and cook over a medium heat for 4–5 minutes until softened. Stir in the garlic and cook for just a minute, then add the chicken and brown all over for a few minutes. Increase the heat to high, add the sherry and bubble for a minute until reduced, then lower the temperature.

Place the saffron in a jug with the hot chicken stock. Stir the rice into the pan and mix well with the chicken and onions, then pour over the stock and stir in the raisins. Cook for 20 minutes until almost all of the liquid has been absorbed by the rice.

Stir in the pine nuts, lemon zest and juice and season to taste with a pinch of salt and pepper. Stir through the parsley and serve immediately.

NUTRITIONAL INFO PER SERVING:
553 CALORIES
39g PROTEIN
61g CARBS
17g FAT

Food Diary Barcode:

307
CALORIES
per serving

Pineapple Chicken

PREP TIME: 10 MINS
COOK TIME: 30 MINS
SERVES: 3

200ml pineapple juice
1½ tbsp sesame oil
40ml reduced-salt soy sauce
500g chicken breast, cubed
160g pineapple (fresh or tinned),
   diced
1 tbsp sesame seeds
Fresh coriander, roughly chopped

This recipe is a winner if you love sweet and savoury dishes. The hero of our recipe is the pineapple, which is used twice. First, the pineapple juice serves as the base of our marinade, providing a sweet and tangy flavour that pairs beautifully with the chicken. Then pineapple chunks are added to the recipe itself, delivering bursts of juicy sweetness that contrast and balance the savoury notes from the chicken and soy sauce. All in all, this recipe is a great way to bring a bit of tropical flair to your midweek dinner table.

Mix the pineapple juice, sesame oil and soy sauce together in a large bowl, then add the cubed chicken breast and let it marinate for at least 30 minutes in the fridge.

Place a frying pan over a medium-high heat. Remove the chicken from the marinade and then pan-fry, in batches if necessary, for about 5 minutes each side until browned all over. Pour over the marinade left in the bowl, then lower the heat and cook for 10 more minutes, or until the chicken is fully cooked. Remove from the heat and add the diced pineapple.

Serve the chicken breast topped with the sesame seeds and fresh coriander.

NUTRITIONAL INFO PER SERVING:
307 CALORIES
39g PROTEIN
13g CARBS
11g FAT

Food Diary Barcode:

Scan here for the
recipe video

292
CALORIES
per serving

Trinidadian Chicken Curry

PREP TIME: 15 MINS,
PLUS MARINATING
COOK TIME: 30 MINS
SERVES: 4

600g chicken thigh fillets
1 tsp coconut oil
1 onion, finely chopped
5g minced garlic
5g minced ginger
1 red chilli pepper, deseeded
and finely chopped (Scotch
Bonnet if you can handle it)
1 tsp curry powder (preferably
a Caribbean blend)
500ml chicken stock
Coriander leaves, to garnish

For the green seasoning
2 spring onions
Handful of fresh coriander
Few sprigs of fresh thyme
(or 1 tsp dried thyme)
5g minced garlic
5g minced ginger
1 red chilli pepper, deseeded
and finely chopped (Scotch
Bonnet if you can handle it)
30ml water
15ml lemon juice
1 tsp curry powder (preferably
a Caribbean blend)

Immerse yourself in the vibrant essence of the Caribbean with this Trinidadian curry, a dish that's one of my favourites in this book! The secret lies in the green seasoning that marinates the chicken, infusing it with layers of flavour. Slowly simmered to tender perfection, this curry is a luscious blend of tradition and taste, capturing the spirited soul of Trinidadian cuisine.

Place all ingredients for the green seasoning in a blender or food processor and process until you have a smooth paste. If it's too thick, add a little more water to help it blend.

Put the chicken thigh fillets into a large bowl and pour the blended green seasoning over them. Allow them to marinate in the fridge for at least 2 hours, or preferably overnight.

When you are ready to cook, heat the coconut oil in a large pan over a high heat. Add the marinated chicken thighs and fry for a couple of minutes each side to brown, then remove from the pan and set aside.

Add the onion to the same pan, reduce the heat to medium-high and fry for a few minutes. Add the garlic, ginger, chilli pepper and curry powder and fry for a further 30 seconds. Add the chicken back to the pan along with the chicken stock.

Cover and let simmer for 10 minutes, then remove the lid and simmer for a further 10 minutes to allow the sauce to thicken and for the chicken to fully cook through.

Serve scattered with coriander leaves.

NUTRITIONAL INFO PER SERVING:
292 CALORIES
30g PROTEIN
7g CARBS
16g FAT

Food Diary Barcode:

366
CALORIES
per serving

Kung Pao Turkey

PREP TIME: 10 MINS
COOK TIME: 15 MINS
SERVES: 3

1 tbsp coconut oil
500g turkey breast, cubed
1 red pepper, chopped
2 red chillies, finely chopped
20g minced garlic
20g minced ginger
4 spring onions, sliced, plus extra
     to garnish
50g unroasted peanuts

For the sauce
3 tbsp soy sauce
1 tbsp cornflour
1 tbsp honey
1 tbsp rice vinegar or white wine
     vinegar
100ml water

This delicious, high-protein fakeaway recipe tastes better than anything you'll get at the local takeaway. It's sweet, spicy and on the plate in under 15 minutes, plus it's cheaper and lower in calories. Not to mention the added satisfaction you get from knowing you made it!

Mix together the ingredients for the sauce and set aside.

Heat the coconut oil in a wok, add the turkey pieces and fry until cooked through. Once cooked, remove from the pan and set aside.

Add the red pepper, chillies, garlic, ginger, spring onions and peanuts to the wok and cook for 2–3 minutes. Return the turkey to the pan along with the sauce, stir to combine and simmer for 3–5 minutes until the sauce has thickened slightly.

Serve with rice and scatter over some more sliced spring onion.

NUTRITIONAL INFO PER SERVING:
366 CALORIES
43g PROTEIN
17g CARBS
14g FAT

Food Diary Barcode:

Scan here for the
recipe video

297
CALORIES
per serving

Turkey Satay

PREP TIME: 5 MINS
COOK TIME: 15 MINS
SERVES: 4

1 tbsp coconut oil
10g minced ginger
10g minced garlic
1 red chilli, finely chopped
500g turkey steaks, sliced
100g baby corn
4 spring onions, sliced
100g mangetout
2 tbsp crunchy peanut butter
1 tbsp fish sauce
150ml water
Black pepper

I'm going to show you how to make a super quick satay recipe that will whisk you off to a Thai street-food market in less than 15 minutes. I mean it when I say it – this dish is ready in under 15 minutes. We're cooking against the clock and winning every time. Think tender turkey, crispy veggies and a tantalising peanut sauce – a combo that promises a flavour explosion with every bite.

Heat the coconut oil in a frying pan or wok over a medium-high heat.

Add the ginger, garlic and chilli (use more or less chilli depending on how hot you like it) and gently fry for 1 minute.

Add the sliced turkey and cook for about 10 minutes until cooked through. Add the baby corn, spring onions and mangetout and cook for a further 2–3 minutes.

Add the peanut butter, fish sauce and water and continue to cook, stirring to mix everything through for a couple of minutes. Season with black pepper to taste and serve.

NUTRITIONAL INFO PER SERVING:
297 CALORIES
37g PROTEIN
8g CARBS
13g FAT

Food Diary Barcode:

Scan here for the
recipe video

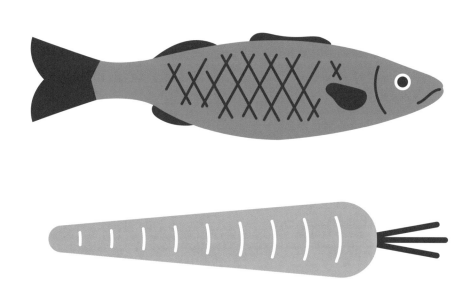

3

FISH & VEG

533
CALORIES
per serving

Chilli Prawn, Chicken & Egg Fried Rice

PREP TIME: 10 MINS
COOK TIME: 15 MINS
SERVES: 4

2 tbsp groundnut oil
2 large free-range eggs, beaten
300g chicken thigh fillets,
   cubed or cut into strips
1 large carrot, cut into thin strips
Bunch of spring onions, chopped
10g minced ginger
10g minced garlic
1 red chilli, finely chopped
165g raw jumbo prawns
100g frozen peas
2 x 250g pouches of jasmine rice
2 tbsp soy sauce
1 tsp fish sauce

Whip up this sizzling dish and bring a burst of flavour to your family dinner table. In just 25 minutes, you'll transform everyday ingredients into a protein-packed feast, complete with the zing of fresh chilli and the warmth of ginger. This recipe is a fantastic way to sneak in veggies for the kids and provide a hearty, nutritious meal for everyone. Quick to prepare and even quicker to disappear – it's a sure-fire winner!

Heat a teaspoon of the oil in a wok over a medium heat, swirling it around to cover the base. Add half of the beaten egg and swirl it around the base of the wok so that it creates a very thin layer. Give it a few seconds (it takes very little time to cook at all), then flip it over to cook the other side, again for just a few seconds. Remove the thin omelette from the pan and set aside. Repeat with the remaining egg for another thin omelette. Once cooled slice both omelettes into thin strips.

Heat a tablespoon of oil in the wok, then add the chicken and carrot strips and cook quickly, stirring around the pan until browned. Add the spring onions, ginger, garlic and chilli and toss everything together to cook for a few minutes.

Add the prawns and peas and cook for a minute, then transfer everything from the wok to a bowl and set aside.

Add the remaining oil to the wok and add the rice. Press the rice down and cook so it is lightly browned on one side then turn it over and brown the other side.

Add the soy sauce and fish sauce to the rice and stir-fry until the rice is completely warmed through. Return all the other ingredients to the wok, mix thoroughly and cook for a final 3 minutes until everything is heated through.

NUTRITIONAL INFO PER SERVING:
533 CALORIES
35g PROTEIN
51g CARBS
21g FAT

Food Diary Barcode:

444 CALORIES per serving

Orzo with Prawns, Tomato & Feta

PREP TIME: 15 MINS
COOK TIME: 25 MINS
SERVES: 4

2 tbsp olive oil
1 onion, finely chopped
15g minced garlic
1 red chilli, finely chopped
200g orzo pasta
1 x 400g tin of finely chopped
   tomatoes
2 tbsp sundried tomato paste
500ml vegetable stock
150g kale, chard or spinach
   leaves, chopped
200g raw jumbo prawns
100g feta, crumbled
Zest and juice of ½ lemon
3 tbsp chopped chives
Sea salt and black pepper

Set sail for the Mediterranean with this delicious recipe. It's an effortlessly elegant dish, high in protein and full of vibrant, fresh ingredients – perfect for a midweek dinner that tastes like a weekend treat.

Heat the oil in a large, deep frying pan. Add the onion and cook for 4–5 minutes. Stir in the garlic and red chilli and cook for just a minute.

Stir in the orzo, then tip in the tomatoes, sundried tomato paste and stock and season with a little salt and pepper. Simmer for 8 minutes until the liquid has reduced and the orzo is nearly cooked.

Stir through the green leaves and the prawns and simmer for 2–3 minutes until the greens have wilted and the prawns are pink and cooked through.

Finish the dish by crumbling over the feta and then sprinkling with the lemon zest and juice and chopped chives.

NUTRITIONAL INFO PER SERVING:
444 CALORIES
28g PROTEIN
47g CARBS
16g FAT

Food Diary Barcode:

804
CALORIES
per serving

Miso Mackerel with Stir-Fried Brown Rice, Mushrooms & Cabbage

PREP TIME: 20 MINS
COOK TIME: 30 MINS
SERVES: 2

4 fillets of mackerel
2 tsp maple syrup
2 tbsp white miso
2 tsp mirin
120g brown rice
2 tbsp olive oil
200g chestnut mushrooms, sliced
10g minced garlic
10g minced ginger
1 red chilli, finely chopped
4 spring onions, finely chopped
150g spring greens, shredded
2 tbsp soy sauce

Here mackerel, known for its rich, omega-packed oils, is marinated in a sweet and umami-laden miso glaze, creating a succulent, flavour-packed main dish. The stir-fried rice brings earthy mushrooms and crisp greens into a delicious dance with aromatic garlic, ginger and a kick of chilli.

Lay the mackerel fillets skin side down on a baking tray lined with parchment paper. Mix the maple syrup, miso and mirin together and brush the mixture all over the fish. Leave to marinate while you cook the rice.

Place the rice in a medium saucepan and cover with water. Bring to the boil and simmer for 20 minutes until the rice is cooked and the liquid has been absorbed.

Heat the oil in a large frying pan and cook the mushrooms over a medium-high heat for 8–10 minutes until golden and softened. Stir in the garlic, ginger, chilli, spring onions and greens and cook for a further 5 minutes until the greens have wilted.

Add the rice to the pan and toss well until combined with all the ingredients, then stir through the soy sauce.

Preheat the grill to high. Place the mackerel fillets under the grill and cook for 5–7 minutes, depending on the thickness of the fillets, until the top browns and the fish is cooked through. Serve with the rice.

NUTRITIONAL INFO PER SERVING:
804 CALORIES
34g PROTEIN
68g CARBS
44g FAT

Food Diary Barcode:

Mauritian Prawn Rougaille

PREP TIME: 20 MINS
COOK TIME: 30 MINUTES
SERVES: 4

1 tbsp coconut oil
1 large onion, finely chopped
15g minced garlic
15g minced ginger
2–3 green chillies, thinly sliced
   (adjust according to your
   heat preference)
½ tsp ground turmeric
1 tsp paprika
2 sprigs of thyme, leaves stripped
½ tsp salt
1 x 400g tin of chopped tomatoes
1 tsp lemon juice
Handful of fresh parsley, chopped
250g cooked prawns
Chopped coriander leaves,
   to garnish

For a vibrant meal that's steeped in the flavours of Mauritius, try this delicious prawn rougaille. It uses succulent prawns that are gently simmered in a fragrant tomato sauce enriched with a medley of spices, including the warmth of turmeric and the brightness of paprika. With the herbal notes of thyme, the kick of green chillies and the freshness of lemon juice, each spoonful is a celebration of taste. Garnish with fresh coriander for an extra pop of colour and flavour. It's a simple yet impressive dish that's perfect for a weeknight dinner.

Heat the oil in a large frying pan or wok over a medium heat. Add the onion and sauté until translucent. Stir in the garlic, ginger and green chillies and cook for another 30–60 seconds.

Add the turmeric and paprika and cook for a further 30 seconds, then add the thyme leaves, salt, chopped tomatoes, lemon juice and parsley and simmer for 8–10 minutes until the sauce has thickened and the tomatoes have broken down.

Add the cooked prawns and just bring them up to temperature – you don't need to 'cook' them as they will be at risk of turning rubbery.

Serve garnished with chopped coriander.

NUTRITIONAL INFO PER SERVING:
137 CALORIES
14g PROTEIN
9g CARBS
5g FAT

Food Diary Barcode:

436 CALORIES per serving

Aubergine, Pea & Tamarind Curry

PREP TIME: 20 MINS
COOK TIME: 40 MINS
SERVES: 4

2 large or 3 small aubergines,
 cut into thick chunks
2 tbsp olive oil
1 tbsp fennel seeds
1 tbsp mustard seeds
1 large red onion, finely chopped
10g minced garlic
10g minced ginger
1 red chilli, finely chopped
1 x 400g tin of chopped tomatoes
1 x 400ml tin of coconut milk
2 tbsp tamarind paste
3 tbsp smooth almond butter
250g frozen peas
Large bunch of coriander,
 chopped
Salt and pepper
1 lime, cut into wedges, to serve
3 tbsp Greek-style yoghurt, to
 serve

Tuck into this delicious vegetable curry, a real symphony of flavours that's sure to liven up your dinner routine! With thick chunks of aubergine roasted to perfection and peas adding a burst of green goodness, this dish is not just pleasing to the palate but also packed with protein.

Preheat the oven to 180°C (160°C fan)/350°F/gas 4. Toss the aubergines with half the olive oil and the fennel and mustard seeds. Season well with salt and pepper and then place in a single layer on baking trays – you may need two or three. Roast in the oven for 25 minutes until cooked, golden and caramelised at the edges.

Heat the remaining olive oil in a large saucepan, add the onion and cook for 5–6 minutes until softened. Stir in the garlic, ginger and chilli and fry for just a minute, then add the tomatoes, coconut milk, tamarind paste, almond butter and a splash of water. Simmer for 10–15 minutes to create a thickened sauce. Season to taste with a little salt.

Stir through the peas, roasted aubergine and coriander and simmer for 5 minutes. Serve with a good squeeze of lime juice, a dollop of Greek-style yoghurt and either some brown rice or wholemeal chapatis.

NUTRITIONAL INFO PER SERVING:
436 CALORIES
14g PROTEIN
23g CARBS
32g FAT

Food Diary Barcode:

579
CALORIES
per serving

Cauliflower & Chickpea Crust Pizza with Roasted Butternut Squash, Nduja, Honey & Sage

PREP TIME: 20 MINS
COOK TIME: 30 MINS
SERVES: 4

1 large cauliflower, broken
    into florets, about 750g
    prepared weight
1 x 400g tin of chickpeas, drained
600g butternut squash, cut into
    wedges (leave the skin on)
1 red onion, cut into wedges
2 tbsp olive oil, plus extra
    for drizzling
100g ground almonds
2 large free-range eggs, beaten
6 tbsp passata
1 x 120g ball of mozzarella, cubed
4 tsp nduja
1 tbsp honey
2 tbsp chopped fresh sage leaves
Sea salt and black pepper

Get ready to roll out the 'dough' for a revolutionary pizza, where the traditional meets the extraordinary! This inventive pizza, topped with roasted butternut squash, spicy nduja and with a sweet hint of honey and sage, brings a festival of flavours and textures to your palate. It's a unique twist on a classic, giving you a hearty dose of protein and vibrant veggies. Perfect for pizza night, this dish promises to be a lip-smacking, healthy hit for all!

Preheat the oven to 200°C (180°C fan)/400°F/gas 6. Place the cauliflower florets and chickpeas in a food processor and blitz until coarsely chopped (you might need to do this in two batches). Spread the mixture out over a couple of baking trays in a shallow layer and place in the oven for 10–12 minutes to roast. Toss everything around and roast for a further 5 minutes.

Meanwhile, toss the butternut squash with the red onion and olive oil and a good pinch of salt and black pepper and roast alongside the cauliflower for 15 minutes until starting to turn golden and tender.

Tip the roasted cauliflower and chickpeas into a large bowl and mix with the ground almonds and beaten eggs. Season with salt and pepper to taste.

Line two large baking trays with parchment paper. Divide the cauliflower and chickpea mixture between the trays and spread out to make two round bases each measuring about 23cm across – make them thicker at the edges to form a crust. Bake for 15 minutes until golden brown and starting to crisp at the edges.

Spoon the passata over the cauliflower bases, then top each one with half the butternut squash and red onions. Sprinkle over the cubed mozzarella and dot spoonfuls of nduja over the top along with the honey. Sprinkle with sage and add a drizzle of oil. Bake for 12–15 minutes until the base is cooked through and crusty and the cheese is melted and bubbling.

NUTRITIONAL INFO PER SERVING:
579 CALORIES
31g PROTEIN
35g CARBS
35g FAT

Food Diary Barcode:

276
CALORIES
per serving

Greek Lentil Soup

PREP TIME: 10 MINS
COOK TIME: 50 MINS
SERVES: 5

2 x 400g tins of brown or
    green lentils
1 tbsp olive oil
1 large onion, finely chopped
2 medium carrots, diced
2 stalks celery, diced
15g minced garlic
1.2 litres vegetable or
    chicken stock
1 x 400g tin of chopped tomatoes
1 bay leaf
1 tsp dried oregano
1 tsp dried thyme
2 tbsp red wine vinegar
    or balsamic vinegar
Chopped parsley, to garnish
Sea salt and black pepper

TIP

This is usually served
without blending but
I like my soups smooth,
so I often blitz with a
hand blender before
serving.

Immerse yourself in the flavours of the Mediterranean with this Greek soup, locally known as 'fakes'. The protein-packed lentils, sautéed with a mirepoix of vegetables and simmered in a herby stock, create a comforting bowl that's both earthy and satisfying. And for a truly Hellenic touch, crumble feta over the top and drizzle with olive oil. Whether you enjoy it chunky or puréed smooth, this soup is a loving hug for the soul.

Drain the lentils and rinse in a sieve under running cold water, then set aside.

Heat the olive oil in a large saucepan over a medium heat. Add the onion, carrots, and celery and sauté until the onion becomes translucent and the vegetables start to soften, about 5 minutes. Add the garlic and sauté for another minute until fragrant.

Mix in the lentils, ensuring they're well combined with the vegetables. Add the stock, chopped tomatoes, bay leaf, oregano, thyme and ¼ teaspoon of black pepper.

Bring the mixture to the boil, then reduce the heat to low and let it simmer for about 30–40 minutes, or until the vegetables are soft and cooked through. You can add more water or stock if the soup becomes too thick.

Once the vegetables are cooked, stir in the red wine or balsamic vinegar. Season with salt to taste and remove the bay leaf.

Ladle the soup into bowls and scatter over some chopped parsley. If desired, sprinkle some crumbled feta cheese on top and drizzle with a bit of olive oil for added flavour and richness.

NUTRITIONAL INFO PER SERVING:
276 CALORIES
17g PROTEIN
43g CARBS
4g FAT

Food Diary Barcode:

274
CALORIES
per serving

Homemade Balsamic Baked Beans

PREP TIME: 10 MINS
COOK TIME: 20 MINS
SERVES: 4

2 tbsp olive oil
1 large onion, finely chopped
15g minced garlic
2 tbsp smoked paprika
1 tsp chilli flakes
1 tbsp dried mixed herbs
2 tbsp tomato purée
2 tbsp balsamic vinegar
1 tbsp honey
2 x 400g tins of haricot or
    cannellini beans, drained
1 x 400g tin of chopped tomatoes
Handful of flat-leaf parsley,
    finely chopped
Sea salt

Onions, garlic, tomatoes, cannellini beans and balsamic are the base for these super tasty beans, which are perfect to have on standby in the fridge for a quick breakfast with an egg of your choice!

Heat the olive oil in a saucepan, add the onion and cook over a medium heat for about 4 minutes until softened. Stir in the garlic and cook for just a minute. Stir through the paprika, chilli, herbs and tomato purée and cook for about a minute.

Add the balsamic vinegar, honey, beans and tomatoes and a good pinch of salt. Add a generous splash of water (rinsing out the tin of tomatoes) and simmer for 15–20 minutes until the sauce has thickened and reduced.

Serve the beans as they are or as part of a breakfast/brunch – they also make a good quick supper topped with chopped parsley and an egg of your choice.

TIP

Keep in the fridge in an airtight container for up to 5 days and serve with eggs of your choice, avocado, grilled halloumi and toasted high protein bread (see page 182).

NUTRITIONAL INFO PER SERVING:
274 CALORIES
13g PROTEIN
33g CARBS
10g FAT

Food Diary Barcode:

446
CALORIES
per serving

One-Pot Piri Piri Tofu

PREP TIME: 15 MINS
COOK TIME: 40 MINS
SERVES: 4

1 small onion, cut into quarters
1 red pepper, deseeded
    and quartered
2 Thai red chillies
Zest and juice of ½ lemon
1 tbsp white wine vinegar
2 tsp smoked paprika
½ tsp dried oregano
10g minced garlic (2 cloves)
1 tbsp honey
2 tbsp olive oil
280g firm tofu, cut into cubes
350g cherry tomatoes or
    1 x 400g tin of cherry tomatoes
2 large handfuls of spinach
250g orzo pasta
Small bunch of chives, chopped
Sea salt and black pepper

The blend of smoky paprika, tangy lemon and hot chillies creates a piri piri sauce that's both mouthwatering and memorable. Coupled with the satisfying sweetness of cherry tomatoes and tofu, this dish is a protein-packed wonder. The orzo pasta provides a delightful base, soaking up all the robust flavours, while the spinach adds a fresh, nutritious twist.

Preheat the oven to 180ºC (160ºC fan)/350ºF/gas 4. Place the onion and pepper in a baking tray and roast in the oven for 25 minutes until lightly charred and softened.

Place the roasted peppers and onion in a food processor with the chillies, lemon zest and juice, vinegar, paprika, oregano, garlic and honey and process until smooth, adding a tablespoon of water if it is looking too thick. You want to end up with a thick, smooth paste.

Heat the oil in a heavy-based casserole or large frying pan. Add the tofu and brown all over for a few minutes until crispy and golden. Tip in the tomatoes and fry with the tofu for a minute, then add the piri piri purée and a tablespoon of water. Season with some salt and pepper and cook for 5–6 minutes until the sauce is starting to reduce and the tomatoes are softening. Stir through the spinach leaves.

Meanwhile bring a small saucepan of water to the boil and cook the orzo for 10 minutes until tender. Drain well.

Serve the orzo in individual serving bowls and top each with the piri piri tofu mixture. Serve scattered with chopped chives.

NUTRITIONAL INFO PER SERVING:
446 CALORIES
21g PROTEIN
59g CARBS
14g FAT

Food Diary Barcode:

Avocado & Broad Bean Smash Quesadillas

PREP TIME: 15 MINS
COOK TIME: 25 MINS
SERVES: 2

3 mixed peppers, deseeded
    and cut into wedges
1 red onion, cut into wedges
1 green fresh jalapeño chilli,
    chopped
2 tbsp olive oil
1 tbsp smoked paprika
1 tsp cumin seeds
150g broad beans, fresh or frozen
1 large avocado, peeled
    and stoned
Small bunch of coriander
Zest and juice of ½ lemon
4 seeded flour tortillas
80g Manchego cheese, grated
Sea salt and black pepper

It's a taste fiesta with these quesadillas! Fresh green broad beans and creamy avocado blend into a delightful smash, tucked between seeded tortillas with a generous sprinkle of Manchego cheese. Perfect for a quick lunch or a casual dinner.

Preheat the oven to 180ºC (160ºC fan)/350ºF/gas 4. Place the peppers, red onion and chilli in a roasting tin and toss with the olive oil, smoked paprika and cumin seeds. Place in the oven and roast for 20 minutes until the peppers are lightly charred and softened.

Meanwhile bring a small saucepan of water to the boil, add the broad beans and cook for a few minutes. Drain and then remove the outer skin (although this is not a necessary part of the process if you don't have time). Tip the broad beans into a food processor and pulse until roughly chopped. Add the avocado and pulse again until you have a rough paste. Transfer to a bowl and stir in the coriander, lemon zest and juice, a pinch of sea salt and plenty of ground black pepper.

Lay a tortilla on your work surface and spread some of the broad bean smash over it. Top with a quarter of the roasted peppers and red onions and a quarter of the Manchego. Top with another tortilla, pressing down well.

Place a frying pan over a medium heat and place the quesadilla in the pan. Toast for 2–3 minutes and then flip and toast the other side for a further 3 minutes. If you find it hard to flip the quesadilla, place a plate over the top and flip onto the plate, then slide it back into the pan on the other side. Cut into wedges and serve.

NUTRITIONAL INFO PER SERVING:
791 CALORIES
26g PROTEIN
66g CARBS
47g FAT

Food Diary Barcode:

466 CALORIES per serving

Cauliflower Cheese Topped Spiced Vegetable Pie

PREP TIME: 20 MINS
COOK TIME: 50 MINS
SERVES: 4

2 tbsp olive oil
1 large onion, finely chopped
15g minced garlic
1 large carrot, grated
2 tbsp rosemary leaves, finely chopped
350g mixed mushrooms, roughly chopped
175g green puy lentils
2 tbsp tomato purée
250ml red wine
800ml vegetable stock
Sea salt and black pepper

For the topping
400g potatoes, peeled and cut into large chunks
1 small cauliflower, cut into florets
100ml half-fat crème fraîche
100g reduced-fat Cheddar cheese, grated

Here a rich mushroom and lentil filling is topped with a cheesy cauliflower and potato mash and baked until crispy. Serve with green vegetables for the ultimate family dinner.

Heat the oil in a large saucepan, add the onion and cook over a medium heat for 4–5 minutes until starting to soften. Stir in the garlic, carrot and rosemary leaves and cook for 1 minute. Stir in the mushrooms and cook for 5–8 minutes until they start to brown and soften. Add the lentils and tomato purée and mix everything together well.

Turn the heat up to high, add the red wine and bring to a simmer. Cook for 5 minutes until the liquid reduces, then pour in the stock and simmer for 20 minutes until the lentils are cooked and the liquid has reduced. Season well to taste.

For the topping, place the potatoes in a saucepan, cover with cold water and add a good pinch of sea salt. Bring to the boil and simmer for 15 minutes, then add the cauliflower florets and simmer for a further 10 minutes until the potatoes and cauliflower are really tender. Drain well and return to the pan. Tip in the crème fraîche and grated Cheddar and mash everything together well. Adding a little more seasoning if required.

Preheat the grill to high. Spoon the lentil mixture into a 2-litre ovenproof dish and spoon the potato and cauliflower mixture on top. Place under the grill and cook until golden and crusty, about 10 minutes.

NUTRITIONAL INFO PER SERVING:
466 CALORIES
25g PROTEIN
51g CARBS
18g FAT

Food Diary Barcode:

Mediterranean Bowl

PREP TIME: 15 MINS
COOK TIME: 15 MINS
SERVES: 4

For the tomato quinoa
2 tbsp olive oil
1 small onion, finely chopped
15g minced garlic
Pinch of chilli flakes
1 tsp dried oregano
150g quinoa
1 litre vegetable stock
1 x 400g tin of finely chopped
    tomatoes
2 tbsp sundried tomato paste
1 x 400g tin of chickpeas, drained
Handful of fresh basil,
    roughly chopped
Large handful of spinach leaves,
    chopped
Sea salt and black pepper

For the tzatziki
200g Greek yoghurt
200g cucumber, diced
3 tbsp fresh mint, finely chopped
Juice of ½ lemon

To serve
100g houmous
100g olives
1 cucumber, sliced
40g cherry tomatoes
2 pittas breads, sliced

This delicious tomato quinoa salad with chickpeas and fresh basil is perfect served alongside houmous, olives, tzatziki, cucumber, tomatoes, olives and pitta bread for the ultimate bowl of goodness.

Heat the olive oil in a saucepan and cook the onion over a medium heat for 4–5 minutes until beginning to soften. Stir in the garlic, chilli flakes and oregano and cook for just a minute.

Stir in the quinoa and toss with the onions and spices. Pour in the stock, finely chopped tinned tomatoes, sundried tomato paste and a pinch of salt and pepper. Simmer for 15 minutes until the quinoa is cooked and has absorbed the liquid. Fluff up with a fork, then stir through the chickpeas, basil and spinach leaves until the spinach has wilted.

For the tzatziki, place all the ingredients in a bowl and mix together, seasoning with a pinch of sea salt and some black pepper.

Spoon the quinoa into a bowl along with the tzatziki and serve with houmous, olives, cucumber, cherry tomatoes and pitta. You could even add some grilled halloumi to this.

NUTRITIONAL INFO PER SERVING:
548 CALORIES
26g PROTEIN
66g CARBS
20g FAT

Food Diary Barcode:

Ultimate Egg Sandwich

PREP TIME: 15 MINS
COOK TIME: 7 MINS
SERVES: 2

4 large free-range eggs
1 tbsp capers, roughly chopped
2 tbsp chopped fresh dill
½ tsp Dijon mustard
2 tbsp mayonnaise
50g watercress, roughly chopped
4 slices of wholemeal bread
Sea salt and black pepper

Soft-boiled eggs combined with capers, dill, mustard and watercress take the humble egg sandwich to the next level. It's simple, it's quick and it's utterly delightful – an eggcellent choice for any day of the week!

Put the eggs into a small saucepan and cover with water. Bring to the boil, then reduce the heat and simmer for 6 minutes. Drain the eggs and run under cold running water until cool enough to handle, then remove the shell and chop roughly. Set aside to cool completely.

Add the capers to a bowl with the dill, mustard, mayonnaise and a pinch of sea salt and some pepper and whisk together well. Stir in the eggs and gently mix together.

Use as a sandwich filling with the watercress between sliced wholemeal bread, or serve as an open sandwich on toasted bread topped with watercress.

NUTRITIONAL INFO PER SERVING:
470 CALORIES
24g PROTEIN
35g CARBS
26g FAT

Food Diary Barcode:

Roasted Squash, Cauliflower & Chickpea Galette

PREP TIME: 20 MINS
COOK TIME: 50 MINS
SERVES: 6

For the pastry
150g butter
200g spelt flour, plus extra for
    dusting
100g quick-cook polenta
1 tsp sea salt

For the topping
2 tbsp olive oil, plus extra for
    drizzling
1 tsp ground turmeric
1 tbsp cumin seeds
1 tsp ground ginger
1 small cauliflower, cut into florets
500g butternut squash, cut into
    large pieces
2 red peppers, deseeded and cut
    into wedges
1 x 400g tin of chickpeas, drained
1 medium egg, lightly beaten
1 tbsp miso
2 tbsp tahini
Juice of ½ lemon
20g pistachio nuts
20g pumpkin seeds

NUTRITIONAL INFO PER SERVING:
547 CALORIES
13g PROTEIN
45g CARBS
35g FAT

Food Diary Barcode:

Roasted butternut squash, cauliflower and red peppers, all spiced with the warming notes of turmeric, cumin and ginger, create a rich tapestry of flavours. The chickpeas add a wonderful protein punch, while a drizzle of miso-tahini dressing infuses the dish with a creamy, umami depth. Topped with the crunch of pistachios and pumpkin seeds, this galette is a glorious celebration of wholesome ingredients that come together to offer a feast for the senses.

To make the pastry, start by putting the butter in the freezer for about 20 minutes. Put the flour, polenta and salt into a large bowl and use a box grater to grate the butter into the flour, then swiftly use a knife to stir the butter into the flour and add 3 tablespoons of ice-cold water. Bring the ingredients together to form a dough. Dust the work surface with flour, tip the dough out and gently knead to form a smooth, flat disc of dough. Wrap in cling film and pop in the fridge while you prepare the filling.

Preheat the oven to 200°C (180°C fan)/400°F/gas 6.

Whisk the olive oil and spices together in a large bowl, then tip in the cauliflower, squash and peppers and toss together. Arrange the vegetables in two large roasting tins so that they are in a single layer, then roast in the oven for 25 minutes until golden.

Remove the pastry from the fridge and roll out on a lightly floured surface to a 30cm circle. Place this on a large baking tray and arrange the roasted vegetables in the centre, leaving a 5cm border. Scatter over the chickpeas and drizzle with a little olive oil. Fold the edges of the pastry circle over the vegetables and brush with a little beaten egg. Bake in the oven for 25 minutes until the pastry is cooked and golden.

Meanwhile, mix together the miso, tahini, lemon juice and a splash of water. Drizzle the galette with the miso and tahini dressing and sprinkle over the pistachio nuts and pumpkin seeds.

**439
CALORIES
per serving**

Creamy Butter Bean, Fennel & Cavolo Nero Gratin

PREP TIME: 15 MINS
COOK TIME: 30 MINS
SERVES: 4

2 tbsp olive oil
1 small onion, finely chopped
1 large fennel bulb, thinly sliced
15g minced garlic
200g cavolo nero or spring
   greens, stems finely chopped,
   leaves shredded
1 tsp chilli flakes
660g jar of butter beans
300ml vegetable stock
1 tbsp Dijon mustard
50g Parmesan cheese,
   finely grated
75g oats
25g hazelnuts, finely chopped
Sea salt and black pepper

This hearty main dish has butter beans and greens in a creamy cheese and mustard sauce topped with a breadcrumb and oat topping and extra Parmesan and hazelnuts for crunch. It also makes an excellent side dish.

Preheat the oven to 200ºC (180ºC fan)/400ºF/gas 6. Heat the olive oil in a large frying pan and cook the onion and fennel over a medium heat for about 4–5 minutes until softened, then stir in the garlic and cook for a minute. Add the green stems of the cavolo nero or spring greens and cook for a further 3–4 minutes, then add the shredded leaves, chilli flakes and butter beans, along with the liquid from the jar.

Add the stock, mustard and half of the Parmesan. Season well to taste and cook for 2 minutes. Transfer to a baking dish.

Combine the remaining Parmesan cheese, oats and hazelnuts together to make a topping, then sprinkle this on top in an even layer. Transfer to the oven and bake for 20 minutes until golden brown.

NUTRITIONAL INFO PER SERVING:
439 CALORIES
22g PROTEIN
45g CARBS
19g FAT

Food Diary Barcode:

283
CALORIES
per serving

Lentil Chilli

PREP TIME: 10 MINS
COOK TIME: 55 MINS
SERVES: 4

1 tsp coconut oil
1 large onion, finely chopped
1 red pepper, diced
2 tsp minced garlic
600ml vegetable stock
175g red lentils, rinsed
1 x 400g tin of kidney beans, rinsed and drained (250g drained weight)
2 tbsp tomato purée
1 tbsp balsamic vinegar
1 tsp chilli powder
2 tbsp fajita seasoning
Pinch of black pepper

This vegetarian chilli is hearty and delicious – the perfect dish for a cold winter evening. Made with lentils, vegetables and a variety of spices, it is both filling and nutritious and all for fewer than 300 calories per portion.

Heat the coconut oil in a large pan over a medium heat and add the onion and pepper. Lightly fry for about 5 minutes until the onion starts to turn golden brown. Add the garlic and fry for a further 30 seconds to 1 minute.

Add all of the remaining ingredients, reduce the heat to low, pop a lid on and gently simmer for about 45 minutes. Be sure to stir the pot every 15 minutes or so and add a splash of water if the lentils soak up too much liquid and it starts to get too thick.

Serve with a dollop of sour cream and some spring onions, if liked.

NUTRITIONAL INFO PER SERVING:
283 CALORIES
16g PROTEIN
48g CARBS
3g FAT

Food Diary Barcode:

Scan here for the recipe video

Asparagus, Pea, New Potato & Taleggio Baked Frittata

PREP TIME: 10 MINS
COOK TIME: 25–30 MINS
SERVES: 4

400g new potatoes
6 large free-range eggs,
   lightly beaten
150g Taleggio cheese,
   rind removed, cubed
Large handful of fresh basil,
   chopped
100g frozen peas, defrosted
200g fresh asparagus spears,
   trimmed

To serve
50g rocket leaves
Juice of ½ lemon
1 tbsp extra virgin olive oil
Pinch of sea salt

This is made in a shallow casserole dish or a roasting tin and baked in the oven for the simplest of suppers. It's delicious served at room temperature, cut into wedges with a crispy green salad. Taleggio is a creamy, flavourful cheese which melts beautifully in this frittata but if you can't get hold of Taleggio then Camembert or Brie work really well too.

Preheat the oven to 180°C (160°C fan)/350°F/gas 4. Place the potatoes in a medium saucepan and cover with water. Bring to the boil and cook for 7 minutes until tender. Drain and allow to cool.

When the potatoes are cool enough to handle, use a sharp knife to slice them into rounds about the thickness of a pound coin.

Add the beaten eggs to the potatoes along with the cubes of cheese, most of the basil and all the peas. Gently fold everything together.

Grease and line a 23cm roasting tin (square or round will both work) with parchment paper. Pour the mixture into the tin, then arrange the asparagus spears on top. Place in the oven to cook for 25–30 minutes until set and golden.

Place the rocket leaves and remaining basil in a bowl and toss with the lemon juice, olive oil and a pinch of sea salt. Serve the frittata cut into wedges, with the rocket and basil salad.

NUTRITIONAL INFO PER SERVING:
383 CALORIES
18g PROTEIN
23g CARBS
23g FAT

Food Diary Barcode:

299 CALORIES per serving

Quinoa & Bean Balls

PREP TIME: 20 MINS
COOK TIME: 45 MINS
SERVES: 4

1 x 400g tin of black beans, drained
2 tbsp olive oil
1 small red onion, finely chopped
10g minced garlic
1 tsp dried oregano
1 tsp red pepper flakes
150g cooked quinoa
60g vegetarian Parmesan (if following a vegetarian diet), finely grated
2 tbsp tomato purée
1 tbsp brown miso paste
3 tbsp chopped flat-leaf parsley
Handful of fresh basil, chopped
Sea salt and black pepper

For the sauce
1 tbsp olive oil
10g garlic, sliced
1 x 400g tin of chopped tomatoes
1 tbsp balsamic vinegar

These meat-free 'meatballs' are baked to perfection, with a wonderful flavourful thanks to the blend of Parmesan and fresh herbs. Served with a simple yet rich tomato sauce and the carb of your choice, this meal promises a comforting, high-protein vegetarian feast.

Preheat the oven to 180°C (160°C fan)/350°F/gas 4. Place the drained black beans in a roasting tin, patting them dry with kitchen paper. Roast for 10 minutes until dried out and cracked.

Meanwhile heat half the olive oil in a frying pan, add the onion and cook for 4–5 minutes until softened, then stir in the garlic and cook for a minute. Add the oregano, red pepper flakes and a good pinch of sea salt and mix well. Tip everything into a food processor along with the beans and pulse for just a minute.

Add the quinoa, cheese, tomato purée, miso and herbs (reserve a few herbs to garnish) and pulse again a few times until everything comes together and you have a thickened mixture, but be careful not to over process as you want some texture.

Tip everything into a bowl and then start to shape the balls – you should get approximately 16 balls, each weighing about 40g.

To make the sauce, heat the oil in a large casserole or heavy-based frying pan and cook the garlic over a medium heat for just a minute, without letting it colour. Tip in the chopped tomatoes and bring to a simmer. Season with salt and pepper, add the balsamic vinegar and simmer for 15 minutes.

Heat the remaining tablespoon of oil in the same pan you used to cook the onion and garlic. Fry the balls for just a few minutes all over until golden, then transfer to a roasting tin and cook in the oven for 10–12 minutes.

Add the balls to the sauce and serve with pasta or brown rice, with an extra sprinkle of chopped herbs.

NUTRITIONAL INFO PER SERVING:
299 CALORIES
13g PROTEIN
28g CARBS
15g FAT

Food Diary Barcode:

Creamy Coconut Black Beans

PREP TIME: 10 MINS
COOK TIME: 45 MINS
SERVES: 4

4 sweet potatoes
2 tbsp olive oil
1 large onion, finely chopped
10g minced garlic
1 x 400g tin of chopped tomatoes
2 tbsp hot chilli sauce
1 x 400ml tin of coconut milk
2 x 400g tins of black beans,
    drained
30g pack of fresh coriander,
    roughly chopped
Sea salt and black pepper

Make a delicious and simple tomato and coconut milk sauce, adding hot chilli sauce to give a delicious depth of flavour, then simply add tinned black beans and simmer until thick and creamy. Serve on baked sweet potatoes and top with coriander – a fantastic alternative to the standard jacket potato and good for vegans too!

Preheat the oven to 200ºC (180ºC fan)/400ºF/gas 6. Pierce the skin of the potatoes with a fork and rub each one all over with a little of the oil. Place on a tray in the oven and bake for 25–35 minutes, depending on size, until very tender.

Meanwhile, heat the remaining oil in a large frying pan and cook the onion for 5–8 minutes until starting to soften. Stir in the garlic and cook for a further few minutes. Tip in the tomatoes, hot sauce, coconut milk and beans, season to taste and bring to a simmer. Cook for 10–15 minutes until the sauce is thickened, reduced and creamy. Check the seasoning and stir through the coriander.

Split the sweet potatoes open and mash and fluff up the flesh with a fork. Spoon over the beans and serve immediately.

NUTRITIONAL INFO PER SERVING:
504 CALORIES
14g PROTEIN
58g CARBS
24g FAT

Food Diary Barcode:

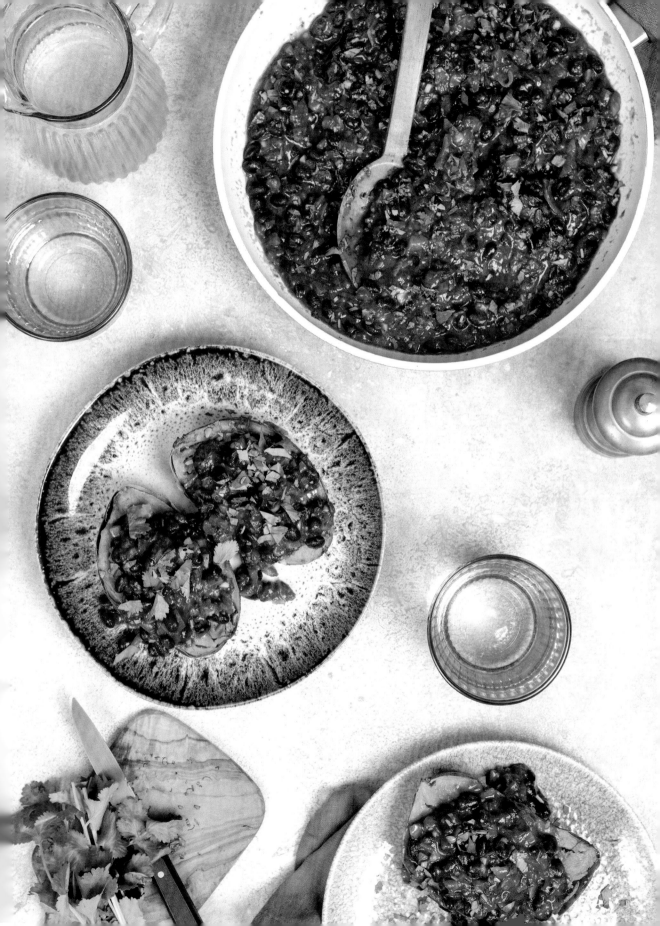

435
CALORIES
per serving

Smoky Tofu Chilli

PREP TIME: 15 MINS
COOK TIME: 35 MINS
SERVES: 4

2 tbsp olive oil
1 large onion, finely chopped
20g minced garlic
20g minced ginger
1 red or green chilli, finely chopped
1 red pepper, chopped
1 tbsp smoked paprika
1 tbsp chilli powder
1 tbsp cumin seeds
2 tbsp chipotle paste
150g green puy lentils
2 x 400g tins of chopped
   tomatoes
800ml vegetable stock
280g firm tofu, patted dry, cut into
   4cm cubes
1 x 400g tin of black beans,
   drained,
Large bunch of coriander, roughly
   chopped

Quick to prepare and delightful to share, this plant-based chilli is a perfect midweek staple for those seeking a satisfying, high-protein vegan feast. It's guaranteed to be a hit with anyone looking to spice up their meal routine without the added fuss!

Add half the oil to a large saucepan and gently soften the onion, garlic, ginger, chilli and red pepper for about 10 minutes.

Add the paprika, chilli powder and cumin seeds and stir around in the pan for a couple of minutes. Stir in half of the chipotle paste, then add the green lentils, chopped tomatoes and stock and simmer for 10 minutes until you have a thickened and reduced sauce and the lentils are nearly cooked.

Meanwhile, toss the tofu in the remaining chipotle paste and heat the remaining oil in a frying pan over a medium heat. Add the tofu and cook for 5 minutes until golden.

Stir the tofu into the sauce along with the black beans. Simmer for 10 minutes, adding a little more stock if the chilli starts to look a bit dry. Stir through the coriander, then serve however you like you chilli – soured cream, grated Cheddar, avocado salsa, tortilla chips, slaw and extra chilli sauce are all good options!

NUTRITIONAL INFO PER SERVING:
435 CALORIES
28g PROTEIN
47g CARBS
15g FAT

Food Diary Barcode:

Red Lentil & Aubergine Moussaka

PREP TIME: 20 MINS
COOK TIME: 45 MINS
SERVES: 6

2 tbsp olive oil, plus extra
   for brushing
1 large onion, finely chopped
2 garlic cloves (10g), thinly sliced
4 sprigs of fresh thyme,
   leaves picked
1 tbsp dried oregano
½ tsp ground cinnamon
1 tbsp tomato purée
150g red lentils
1 x 400g tin of chopped tomatoes
800ml vegetable stock
4 tbsp chopped flat-leaf parsley
2 large aubergines, thinly sliced
500g sweet potatoes, thinly sliced
250g ricotta cheese
300ml crème fraîche
50g vegetarian Parmesan
   (if following a vegetarian diet),
   finely grated
Sea salt and black pepper

This recipe brings the essence of the Mediterranean to your table in just over an hour. It's a protein-rich, comforting bake that's perfect for a family dinner or a special weekend treat, promising satisfaction in every delicious, healthy forkful.

Preheat the oven to 200ºC (180ºC fan)/400ºF/gas 6.

Heat the oil in a medium saucepan, add the onion and cook over a medium heat for 4–5 minutes until starting to soften. Add the garlic, thyme, oregano and cinnamon and cook for 1 minute. Stir in the tomato purée and red lentils and cook for a further minute, then tip in the chopped tomatoes, stock, a teaspoon of salt and some pepper. Bring to a simmer and cook for 20 minutes until the lentils are cooked and the liquid has nearly all been absorbed. Stir through the chopped parsley.

Meanwhile, arrange the aubergine and sweet potato slices on baking trays in a single layer and brush with olive oil. Bake in the oven for 15–20 minutes until the slices are browned and softened.

Spoon half the lentil sauce into the base of an ovenproof dish measuring 20 x 30cm, then layer over half the potato and aubergine slices. Top with the remaining lentils, then sweet potato slices, then finish with a layer of aubergines.

Put the ricotta into a bowl with the crème fraîche and grated cheese and spoon over the aubergines, smoothing out to cover the top. Bake in the oven for 20–25 minutes until heated through and golden brown. Serve the moussaka cut into wedges with a crisp salad on the side, if liked.

NUTRITIONAL INFO PER SERVING:
459 CALORIES
14g PROTEIN
40g CARBS
27g FAT

Food Diary Barcode:

4

SNACKS & DESSERTS

445
CALORIES
per serving

Berry, Pear & Mixed Seed Crisp

PREP TIME: 15 MINS
COOK TIME: 25 MINS
SERVES: 6

350g mixed fresh or frozen berries
    (defrosted if frozen)
4 medium pears, peeled,
    cored and chopped
75g light muscovado sugar
Grated zest and juice of
    1 small orange
75g ground almonds
75g porridge oats
4 tbsp mixed seeds
75g coconut oil, melted

Embrace the sweetness and nutritional benefits of this dessert – a yummy blend of soft, juicy fruits and a crunchy, nutty topping that's wonderfully wholesome. With a high-protein twist from the seeds and almonds, and a gratifying crunch from the oats, this crisp is an absolute delight, served warm with a dollop of yoghurt for that perfect finish. Although it's perhaps not particularly 'calorie friendly' it certainly is delicious . . .

Preheat the oven to 200ºC (180ºC fan)/400ºF/gas 6. Place the mixed berries in a 1.2 litre ovenproof dish along with the chopped pears. Stir in half the sugar and the orange zest and juice.

Place the remaining sugar in a bowl and add the almonds, oats and mixed seeds. Stir through the coconut oil, making sure everything is coated in the oil.

Pile the mixture on top of the fruit and bake in the hot oven for 25 minutes until the top is golden and the fruit is bubbling at the edges.

Serve warm with a dollop of Greek or coconut yoghurt.

NUTRITIONAL INFO PER SERVING:
445 CALORIES
8g PROTEIN
47g CARBS
25g FAT

Food Diary Barcode:

197
CALORIES
per serving

Nut & Seed Bread

PREP TIME: 20 MINS
COOK TIME: 45 MINS
MAKES: 18 SLICES

7g sachet of dried yeast
2 tbsp extra virgin olive oil
1 tsp honey
250g gram (chickpea) flour
100g ground almonds
30g ground flaxseeds
100g mixed seeds, such as
    linseeds, chia, poppy, sunflower
    and pumpkin
60g walnuts, roughly chopped
60g cashews, roughly chopped
1 tsp sea salt
4 large free-range eggs

**For your ultimate egg, avocado, bean or houmous sandwich –
a simple bread made with yeast, gram flour, ground almonds,
mixed seeds, nuts and eggs.**

Preheat the oven to 180°C (160°C fan)/350°F/gas 4. Line a 1.5-litre
loaf tin with parchment paper.

Fill a jug with 400ml of warm water and add the yeast, oil and
honey. Mix together and set aside for 10 minutes until the surface
of the liquid is foamy with small bubbles. This means the yeast
has been activated.

Meanwhile put the flour, ground almonds and all the seeds
and nuts into a large bowl with the sea salt and mix until well
combined.

Whisk the eggs into the yeast mixture. Pour the whole lot into
the flour, nut and seed mix and stir together well until you have
a smooth, thick batter. Pour into the prepared tin.

Bake for 45 minutes until golden and a skewer inserted into
the centre comes out clean. Transfer to a wire rack to cool.

TIP
———
This will keep well for
up to 4 days in an
airtight container –
it's perfect toasted.

NUTRITIONAL INFO PER SLICE:
197 CALORIES
7g PROTEIN
13g CARBS
13g FAT

Food Diary Barcode:

215
CALORIES
per serving

Chocolate & Date Bars

PREP TIME: 10 MINS
MAKES: 12 BARS

100g raw cashews
175g pitted medjool dates
50g almond or peanut butter
25g maple syrup
30g coconut flour
30g shredded or
    desiccated coconut
1 tsp almond extract
2 tbsp coconut oil

For the topping
100g dark chocolate
1 tsp coconut oil

This is such a delicious, sweet treat: cashews, dates, nut butter and coconut are blitzed in a food processor to create the tastiest filling, which is then pressed into a tin and topped with melted chocolate. Everything is then chilled and cut into bars for the perfect treat. Although not particularly high in protein, they are ridiculously good.

Place the cashews in a food processor and blitz until coarsely ground. Add the remaining ingredients except the chocolate and coconut oil for the topping and blitz until you have a fairly smooth mixture. Press into a 20cm square cake tin.

To make the topping, place the chocolate and the coconut oil in a heatproof bowl and set over a pan of gently simmering water (making sure the base of the bowl doesn't touch the water). Allow to melt, stirring every now and then. Alternatively, melt in a microwave-safe bowl in the microwave on high, in 30-second bursts, until melted.

Spread over the top of the filling and chill until set. Cut into bars.

TIP

Freeze the bars individually so you have them to hand when the sweet need hits!

NUTRITIONAL INFO PER SERVING:
215 CALORIES
4g PROTEIN
16g CARBS
15g FAT

Food Diary Barcode:

Squidgy Pistachio & Raspberry Brownies

PREP TIME: 15 MINS
COOK TIME: 30 MINS
MAKES: 16

200g dark chocolate
150g unsalted butter
3 large free-range eggs
250g coconut sugar
1 tsp vanilla extract
150g ground almonds
50g pistachio nuts, finely chopped
125g raspberries

Quick to whip up and even quicker to disappear, these squares of joy are a perfect tasty snack or a post-dinner treat. Not even remotely high protein but they taste so good it would have been rude not to include them. Thank me later . . .

Preheat the oven to 180°C (160°C fan)/350°F/gas 4 and grease a 20cm brownie tin with parchment paper.

Put the chocolate and butter into a heatproof bowl and melt gently together over a pan of gently simmering water, making sure the base of the bowl doesn't touch the water. (Alternatively melt in the microwave on high in a couple of 30-second bursts.)

Break the eggs into a separate bowl and beat together with the sugar until pale, light and fluffy, then carefully fold in the vanilla, melted chocolate, ground almonds, half the pistachio nuts and half the raspberries. Spoon into the prepared tin and top with the remaining raspberries and pistachio nuts.

Bake for 25–30 minutes until just cooked, then leave to cool for 20 minutes before removing from the tin. Cool completely before cutting into squares or wedges.

NUTRITIONAL INFO PER SERVING:
297 CALORIES
6g PROTEIN
21g CARBS
21g FAT

Food Diary Barcode:

Index

Acknowledgements

Creating this recipe book would not have been possible without the generous support of many.

First and foremost, I would like to express my sincere thanks to my family, whose love and support have been my constant source of strength, and for never complaining about trying a new stew, curry or something 'fancy' when all they wanted was pizza and chips.

Immense thanks go to Georgie, the skilled photographer, and Nathan, the designer. Their creativity and attention to detail have brought the essence of each recipe to life, turning them into visual feasts.

I am also grateful to Lauren and Liv at Catalyst and Sabhbh, my agent, for their belief in this project. Their guidance and professionalism were crucial in making this book a reality.

A heartfelt appreciation to the kitchen heroes: Angela, Daisy and Alison. Your eagerness to help me create and cook dishes, provide feedback and share in the culinary experience has been invaluable. Your insights and enthusiasm have not only improved these recipes but have also made this journey immensely rewarding.

A shoutout must go to my assistant, Steph, for her tireless efforts and dedication to her work. Steph, your attitude and attention to detail have been indispensable in bringing another book to fruition.

And finally, to every reader, thank you for joining me on this flavourful high-protein adventure. May these recipes add joy and inspiration to your cooking as much as they have to mine. Thank you all for being a part of this story.